Modern Catalan
Literature

Catalan Studies
Translations and Criticism

Josep M. Solà-Solé
General Editor

Vol. 18

PETER LANG
New York • Washington, D.C./Baltimore • San Francisco
Bern • Frankfurt am Main • Berlin • Vienna • Paris

Modern Catalan Literature

Proceedings of the Fourth Catalan Symposium

Josep M. Solà-Solé, Editor

PETER LANG
New York • Washington, D.C./Baltimore • San Francisco
Bern • Frankfurt am Main • Berlin • Vienna • Paris

Library of Congress Cataloging-in-Publication Data

Catalan Symposium (4th: 1993: Catholic University of America)
Modern Catalan literature: proceedings of the Fourth Catalan Symposium/
Josep M. Solà-Solé, ed.
p.   cm. — (Catalan studies; vol. 18)
English and Catalan.
Includes bibliographical references.
1. Catalan literature—History and criticism—Congresses.
I. Solà-Solé, Josep M. (Josep María). II. Title. III. Series.
PC3801.A3C3   849'.909—dc20   95-30239
ISBN 0-8204-2779-9
ISSN 1058-1642

Die Deutsche Bibliothek-CIP-Einheitsaufnahme

Modern Catalan literature: proceedings of the Fourth Catalan Symposium/
Josep M. Solà-Solé, ed. – New York; Washington, D.C./Baltimore; San
Francisco; Bern; Frankfurt am Main; Berlin; Vienna; Paris: Lang.
(Catalan studies; Vol. 18)
ISBN 0-8204-2779-9
NE: Solà-Solé, Josep M. [Hrsg.];
Catalan Symposium <4, 1993, Washington, D.C.>; GT

**Published with the cooperation of the
Institució de les Lletres Catalanes.**

Cover design by James F. Brisson.

The paper in this book meets the guidelines for permanence and durability
of the Committee on Production Guidelines for Book Longevity
of the Council of Library Resources.

© 1995 Peter Lang Publishing, Inc., New York

Printed in the United States of America.

TABLE OF CONTENTS

FOREWORD

Ellen Ginsberg

Chairperson
Modern Languages and Literatures
The Catholic University of America
Washington, DC 20064

These proceedings are the fruit of the IVth Catalan Symposium, which took place on the campus of The Catholic University of America on October 16 and 17, 1993, under the auspices of the Center for Catalan Studies of this institution of higher learning.

The following American and Canadian scholars participated in the IVth Symposium, dedicated to modern and contemporary Catalan literature: Frederic Barberà, University of Toronto; Eulàlia Benejam Cobb, Office of Education, Washington, D.C.; Patricia J. Boehne, Eastern College; Peter Cocozzella, State University of New York at Binghamton; Robert J. González-Casanovas, The Catholic University of America (now at the University of Kentucky); Maria Guasch, University of Guelph, Canada; Edward J. Neugaard, University of South Florida; and Josep M. Solà-Solé, The Catholic University of America, Director of the Symposium.

The topics treated in the IVth Symposium ranged from general studies of modern Catalan poetry (Boehne), to more specific studies on a poet (Cocozzella on Agustí Bartra), a particular poetic composition

(Solà-Solé on "El cant espiritual" by Joan Maragall), a novel (Guasch on *Quilòmetres de tul per a un petit cadàver* by Antònia Vicens, and Gonzàlez-Casanovas on *Raimon o el seny fantàstic* by Lluís Racionero Grau), and to modern Catalan folktales (Neugaard, who, at the same time, presents a complete bibliography of the "rondalla"). The correspondence between two Catalan women writers is analyzed (Benejam Cobb on Mercè Rodoreda and Anna Murià); it discusses the stylistic relationship between the Catalan storyteller Pere Calders, recently deceased, and Julio Cortázar (Barberà).

Parallel to the Symposium, a commemoration of the fiftieth anniversary of the death of Màrius Torres, a celebrated Catalan poet, took place with the recital of some of his poems, in the original Catalan and in its English translation by Francesc M. Franch. A lecture was offered (and it is also published in these proceedings) by Enric Bou, Wellesley College, on the topic "'Silenci en un jardí': Màrius Torres and the Catalan Literary Tradition."

Finally, these proceedings offer extensive translations of works by two contemporary Catalan poets. These translations received a prize in the First Catalan Literary Competition, organized jointly by the Center for Catalan Studies and the Paulí Bellet Foundation. These prizes were awarded at the end of the IVth Catalan Symposium. The first is a translation, undertaken by Elaine M. Lilly, of *Vint-i-set poemes en tres temps (Twenty-Seven Poems: Of Gold, Silver, and Tin)* (1972) by Miquel Martí i Pol (b. 1929). The second is a translation by Hillary J. Gardner, of *Llavis que dancen (Lips that Dance)* (1987) by the woman poet Olga Xirinacs (b. 1936).

These proceedings are a modest sample of the vitality of Catalan studies in the United States and Canada. They also represent the long commitment of The Catholic University of America to Catalan language and culture, which goes back, without interruption, to 1963, when the university was one of the first American institutions of higher learning to offer Catalan language classes on a regular basis.

July, 1994

I. STUDIES

Frederic Barberà

PERE CALDERS' AND JULIO CORTÁZAR'S SHORT STORIES: A COMPARATIVE STUDY

Many critics have dealt with either the narrative voice or the fantastic in Cortázar's short stories; in this way, Mora Valcárcel (1982) made a great effort in distributing most of these short stories by following methodically Genette's narrative categories. Concerning the fantastic element, Eyzaguirre (1986) and Gloria Cruz (1988), both made an attempt to define the nature of the fantastic in Cortázar's short stories taking Todorov's *Le Fantastique* as a starting point. And yet a very important aspect was neglected by such an effective theoretical scaffolding: the different ways in which speech through narrative uttering shapes the fantastic and makes it appear in the text through different devices in such a way that it becomes acceptable for the reader. This is, ultimately, our goal in this approach to Cortázar's short stories, but also to those by Calders to which unfortunately (or fortunately, who knows) critics have not paid as much attention.

* * *

In the case of Cortázar's short stories, many different dicursive devices, the result of which is the objectivization of the fantastic, carry out a progressive acceptance of this element in the minds of the readers. In this way, those deliberate attempts of empiric observation which come through the narrative voice already in the very first realistic novels, now emerge in these short stories to make the fantastic more and more credible. This is the case of explicative interpolations like this,

> (nunca sabremos como)
> > ("Queremos tanto a Glenda")

or the recurrent use of adverbs or periphrasis of doubt, which ends up by showing the limitations of a human narrator when trying to give an empirical version of a whole set of odd facts.

> *Quizá* el apetito fue la razón dominante,...
> > ("Reunión con un círculo rojo")

> ...y supongo que gritaba como las demás, *probablemente* como yo mismo.
> > ("Las ménades")

> *Debió durar* un segundo, *acaso* algo más...
> > ("Los pasos en las huellas")

Likewise, the use of disjunction by the narrative voice would have a similar effect.

> ...para completar un pedido *o* acaso cambiarlo *o* irse,
> > ("Reunión con un círculo rojo")

And even sometimes a special treatment of the linguistic register being used by the narrative voice can work its way to making a very peculiar situation appear as pure routine. This is the case of the following narrative statement:

> A las cinco de la mañana...los pongo en el armario y hago la limpieza.
> > ("Carta a una señorita de París")

where the 1st person narrator is referring to a few live rabbits that he has just nicely vomited. Furthermore some other discursive devices make the fantastic elements become accepted by the reader not through objectivization but through bringing it nearer to him. Thus the use of adverbs the nature of which is meant to be closer to reality often comes up in the text together with the 1st narrative person and the present tense to shape different levels of reality in the fiction of the same short story. This is the effect which would come up in the reading of this passage in "Botella al mar"

...mientras *yo aquí* termin*o esta* carta y usted en algún lado,...

where the 1st person "yo," the adverb "aquí," the present tense "termino" and even the demonstrative "esta" work out a "more real" level of fiction in the mind of the reader in a very subtle way which is to be distinguished from the other level pointed to as more distant, more vague, by the same narrator, "usted," "en algún lado," ... and more "unreal" as a result. And sometimes only a difference of aspect within the past tense would be enough to establish two different "realities" within the fantastic; so it occurs in the following passage of "El otro cielo":

...y Josiane *fue* otra vez mía en su bohardilla

... Pero *helaba* en las calles, y las noticias de la guerra...

where that switch of verbal aspect is the only subtle evidence that brings the reader, along with the narrator's experiences, from 1870 Paris to early 1940s Buenos Aires.

In spite of the importance of all these different discursive devices allowing the fantastic to become either more objective or closer to the reader, many more devices of the same discursive nature are to be found in Cortázar's short stories producing ambiguity and, along with it, creating an ideal context for the fantastic to come up. This ambiguity can be achieved in different ways. Thus those devices that cause vagueness are used quite often with this purpose, from variations purely morphological that deliberately make it impossible for the reader to know about the gender of a very odd community

> un*o* de nosotros..., la otr*a*...
> (un*a* de nosotros prepara...)
>
> un*o* de nosotros se ocupa del apare...

in "Cefalea," to the use of vague demonstratives, both adjectives and pronouns

> ...que nunca le habían querido, que había *esa* enfermedad,...
>
> ...para librarse de *eso* que seguía aferrando la garganta de Dina,...

in "Cuello de gatito negro" where, because of them, the reader cannot figure out anything specific; to the use of substantives the meaning of which is so generic that in a general context of deliberate confusion it does not give the reader any precise information about any thing. In this way, again in "Cefalea," we never get to know the misterious job the members of that strange community were doing since it is always referred to as "la tarea,"

> ... si *la tarea* espera en los corrales

and the same happens when the reader tries to know more about the way of life of the community itself, as the set of rules they are meant to follow is always referred to as "el estatuto."

> ... sin previo aviso, sin cumplir para nada *el estatuto*, se han ido anoche los muy hijos de puta,...

Another source of ambiguity is to be found in the deliberate absence of the parts of the sentence, along with the lack of expected information which that represents for the reader; we find a whole paradigm of these "absences" in "Las fases de Severo" where although it is obvious that something of importance is happening around the central character, Severo, we never really get to know what is going on throughout the whole short story, those absences being mainly responsible for it. In this way, when the 1st person narrative voice states

> Me hubiera gustado darle conversación... *para distraerla* [0].

or

> Mamá manda decir que *se preparen.*

we, readers, never get to know "de qué," in the first case, or "para qué," in the second case. Absences, blanks (informative as well as grammatical) that result in an ambiguous understanding in the reading process...once more, the favourable ambience for the fantastic has been created.

In Calders' short stories, the fantastic element, which appears in most of them and gives them form, also meets an effective objectivization through the narrative voice via many discursive devices leading to a progressive "acceptance" by the reader. In this way, the narrator's claims to empirical observation of facts are indeed a good weapon against what otherwise would turn out to be suspected of "fantastic." Thus, a whole set of similar formulas underlining veracity:

> ... del que estava segur era que,...

> ... se m'aparegué com absolutament indubtable.

or paradoxically getting rid of the purely imaginative or literary as
unreliable

> Pot parlar-se aquí d'una força oculta, novelesca,...? No. De cap
> manera.

> ... una superfície de carn neta i viva substituïa el monyó
> sangonós de nervis i de tendons *que algú s'hauria imaginat.*
> (all in "Les mans del taumaturg")

Likewise, stereotyped claims to a unique truth directly opposed to the
apparently fantastic,

> Però la veritat és que...
> ("Triangles màgics")

or to claim to the readers' general knowledge,

> Sabia—*ho sap tothom*—que...
> ("Un estrany al jardí")

or just the recognition of the narrative voice's own ignorance

> No he pogut saber mai si...
> ("Triangles màgics")

> ... què sé jo quins...
> ("Les mans del Taumaturg")

—only as a means of showing the human limits of empirical observation—, all of them are different manifestations of that effective process of
objectivization of the fantastic.

Certainly, there is no doubt that the fantastic element is brought
nearer the reader in an effective way through devices such as the ones we
have mentioned; but it is fair to say that, in Calders' short stories,
neither they nor the recurrent use of the present tense as well as the 1st

narrative person, which often accompanies them, are the main distinctive features of that process of "acceptance" of the fantastic. If in Cortázar, as we saw above, several discursive sources producing ambiguity were mainly responsible for the acceptance of the fantastic, far more than those other devices of objectivization which also existed in his short stories, in the case of Calders, the process of acceptance of the fantastic is mostly carried out, still from objectivization, but through humor and irony. And, also in this case, quite a few discursive devices of different nature are serving this purpose. Thus, on the one hand is the shaping of a peculiar linguistic register through using spontaneous expressions or hilarious reactions when confronting the fantastic.

> No vau preguntar-li *què hi busquen* a la Terra?

—is asked of the narrator of "El millor amic" about an alien whom he has just met; and, likewise, in "Imprevist a la casa número deu," after a terrible gas explosion in the neighbourhood, the narrative voice states:

> Cadascú rep sobre seu el munt de runes *que li pertoca*, amb resignació.

and not long after that:

> [unes veïnes] *aprofiten* el succés per a desmaiar-se

It is often the peculiar linguistic register in charge of bringing along a dissonant element which clashes humorously with the fantastic, particularly when the story is near the end. Thus when, at the end of "El millor amic" the man who met an alien reaches the conclusion that the reason why they do not come very often to Earth is because they are afraid of dogs; this being said in colloquial Catalan sounds rather hilarious.

> ... que els gossos els fan por. ... aquesta és la causa que no baixin més sovint!

On the other hand, some other discursive devices come up in the text through metaliterary remarks such as the following ones the apparent result of which is the parody of what is being narrated, which in this story, "Un estrany al jardí," is the appearance of a talkative soul in the garden of the narrator's friend.

> Però això requereix no tan sols un punt i a part, sinó un espai generós marcat amb asteriscos.

> ... quant al curs de la present història, també ha arribat el moment d'obrir un a part final, amb un nou espai que remarqui la seqüència.

In the same way, a similar effect is achieved by the use of contrast, by juxtaposing solemn elements to hilarious actions often translated into slang terms, for instance when the narrator-character of "Un estrany al jardí" tells us about the moment when he realized that his wife was digging near where he had just found an egiptian mummy in the garden of his old Catalan "masia," he does so in the following terms,

> Vet aquí que un dia me la vaig trobar furgant en *la parcel·la de la mòmia.*

—where the use of the word "furgar," mainly used in a low register meaning "to scrape inside one's nose" applied to an ancient mummy who, like 20th century urban citizens in Catalonia, owns a "parcel·la" (a piece of land for building purposes), all together has an immediate parodic effect on the poor mummy, but, implicitely, the same device has further implications: we, readers, even though we laugh at the poor mummy, get to believe that it is likely for an Egiptian mummy to be found in Catalonia buried in somebody's garden, as we before got to believe that a talkative soul was having a chat in somebody else's garden, or that aliens, even though they are afraid of dogs, may come to Earth from time to time.

Cortázar's and Calders' short stories: two different sides of the fantastic through narrative uttering.

Dept. of Spanish and Portuguese
University of Toronto
Ontario, CANADA M5S 1J4

Eulàlia Benejam Cobb

MAIMED BY LOVE:
MERCÈ RODOREDA'S LETTERS TO ANNA MURIÀ

Mercè Rodoreda died in 1983 in her native Catalonia, at the age of 74. At the time of her death, she had achieved recognition as the principal figure in contemporary Catalan letters, and her novels and stories had been translated to more than fifteen languages. In 1985, a Catalan women's publishing house brought out the writer's correspondence with Anna Murià from 1939 to 1956.

The letters, which have not yet been translated into English, were written by Rodoreda from her exile in France and Switzerland. In these hastily-written notes, prompted sometimes by hunger but mostly by amorous despair, the fiercely ambitious and ego-centered Rodoreda depends for her moral survival on the unstinting support of Anna Murià, herself a writer who subordinated her career to that of her lover, the poet Agustí Bartra.

The interplay of Murià and Rodoreda—one desperately unhappy in love but determined and ultimately triumphant as an artist; and the other, "happy" in her traditional female sacrifice and forever overshadowed by the man she loved—reveals with striking clarity the dilemma of the woman artist. The letters merit attention because, despite their spontaneous and non-literary quality, they bring to the fore the drama of the woman genius, the "...violence of the poet's heart when caught and tangled in a woman's body" (Woolf 50).

In telling the story of Mercè Rodoreda one is hampered by a dearth of biographical materials. Five years after Rodoreda's death, Barcelona's bookstores did not offer a single biography of the writer, even though her fiction is more popular than ever. All that is available to the scholar at present are the biographical snippets included in criticism of her work or in the dust jackets of her novels.

Perhaps this absence of personal information is a form of amends for past excesses. A 1937 article written after Rodoreda's novel *Aloma* won the Creixells Prize (Burbano 122) devotes one third of its length to a discussion of her physical appearance, and coyly adds, at the end, a warning to potential admirers that the writer is married, and has an eight-year-old son.

The author of the article does refrain from mentioning, however, that at the time Rodoreda was separated from her husband, whom she had married at nineteen, and that he—the husband—was her mother's brother. In 1939 her personal life took an even more unconventional turn as, on the eve of the entrance of the Franco forces into Barcelona, Rodoreda fled to France with a truckload of Catalan intellectuals, leaving her child behind with her mother. She did not see him for another ten years.

Mercè Rodoreda and Anna Murià had first met each other in the journalistic and literary milieu of pre-war Barcelona. But their intimacy began in earnest at the castle of Roissy, an *auberge de jeunesse* near Paris where the refugees were housed until the German invasion in 1940. There they shared a room and an adventure. For it was in that idyllic castle with its surrounding gardens and woods that both women fell in love, Anna Murià with the poet Agustí Bartra, and Rodoreda with Armand Obiols, a writer and editor who also had left his family behind.

Murià and Bartra were both single, and their relationship caused no scandal. But the Obiols-Rodoreda affair instantly divided the refugees into two violently opposing camps—those who championed family fidelity, and those who approved of the new passion. Although Murià was one of Rodoreda's supporters, she may have had forebodings of disaster for her friend, for when she and Bartra left France for the Dominican Republic in early 1940 she begged Rodoreda to go with them. But Rodoreda chose to stay in France with Obiols, and that is how the correspondence began.

Anna Murià soon left the Dominican Republic for Mexico, where she bore Bartra's son and daughter, wrote magazine articles and children's stories, and devoted herself to nurturing what she believed to be his genius. In the dust jacket of her 1975 tribute to his writing, *L'obra de Bartra*, Murià mentions that before she left Spain she published two novels of which she is now ashamed, that she has two children of whom she is proud, and that she is putting the finishing touches on a novel that she has been writing, intermittently, for the last twenty years. A personal note: I met Anna Murià and Agustí Bartra at Yale in 1980, and visited them in their home in Catalonia the following summer. It was not until the end of that visit, when she silently handed me a copy of her book, that I realized that she, too, was a writer. She appeared to me throughout our acquaintance as her husband's shadow, always at his side, hardly ever speaking, fetching drinks and books with a smile.

The Rodoreda correspondence includes one letter from Anna Murià dated May 30, 1940. It never reached Rodoreda, who was fleeing Paris because of the German invasion, and was returned to Murià. The letter presents a remarkable mixture of utter abnegation and profound happiness: "All the wonders of the world are not worth the wonder of love fulfilled..." [This and all subsequent Catalan-English translations are my own] she writes. Her greatest joy in exile was the day when Bartra gave a reading of his poems and at the end the organizers gave her a bouquet of flowers. Although, she says, she herself had on many occasions given lectures and been offered flowers, she found it especially thrilling to be honored as "...the poet's lady! I who until now was ensconced in my own personality find it sweet to have become *the extension* (my underline) of a man's personality....I was born to be a wife, Mercè." (Rodoreda, *Cartes* 49)

The profound difference between the temperaments of the two women comes through in the tone of the letters. Murià is maternal and concerned. Already in the Roissy days she nurtured and defended her friend, brought her breakfast in bed and messages from Obiols. Now she sends her words of advice and bags of coffee, and pulls strings to have Rodoreda's stories appear in Catalan magazines published abroad.

If Murià's letters sound maternal, Rodoreda's often exhibit a childish quality. She comes across as self-centered, complaining, demanding. Certainly, her circumstances were very difficult: after the German invasion, when she and her lover fled to Bordeaux, she had to earn a living doing piece-work for a boutique, and the man for whose love she had endured the opprobrium of her compatriots seems to have been an unfortunate choice, a weak and indecisive intellectual who could not bring himself to divorce the wife he had left behind and marry Rodoreda.

Judging from Rodoreda's descriptions of Obiols, La Rochefoucauld is right when he says that, if its effects are any indication, love resembles nothing so much as hate (see Bishop 233). In a bitter letter prompted by a visit to France of Obiols's wife, who was hoping to reconcile herself with her husband, Rodoreda says, "I don't have a rival, Anna. What I really have is an *enemy*, and that enemy is the man I love" (Rodoreda, *Cartes* 84). Rodoreda reveals to her friend that, throughout the long years in Bordeaux when she wore herself out sewing to support herself and her lover, Obiols kept writing encouraging letters to his wife, hinting at an impending reunion. When all is over and done, she assures Murià, "Obiols will be able to boast of having destroyed the life of Mercè Rodoreda" (Rodoreda, *Cartes* 85).

Despite her rage, however, Rodoreda could not bear to part with her lover. When his wife visited him in Bordeaux, Rodoreda fled to Paris vowing never to see him again, only to send him a frantic letter two days later begging for a little love (Rodoreda, *Cartes* 80). After eight years of enduring the torments caused by his indecision, she confesses abjectly that she cannot exist without his physical presence: "Even if love is gone, I can still see him, I still have him near me, I still feel him by my side at night" (Rodoreda, *Cartes* 85).

In another letter, Rodoreda says that she will stop working for the *Revista de Catalunya*, published by exiled Catalans in Paris, because Obiols is jealous of her (Rodoreda, *Cartes* 89). Yet it appears from his critiques of *La Mort i la primavera*, that in the early 1960's he was fully aware of Rodoreda's genius, respected it, and had no qualms about acknowledging it: "In all of Catalan prose I do not believe there is a character as alive as Colometa, nor a village as hallucinating and real as the one in *La Mort*" (see Folch i Pi, "Pròleg," in Rodoreda, *La mort* 7).

Despite what the real truth may have been, Rodoreda's perception of her relationship with Obiols was one of unallayed misery, and she was well aware of the degradation that this enslavement implied. Less than a year after the beginning of the affair she writes, "And from so much crying on the days when I am alone, I no longer feel pity for myself, but disgust."(Rodoreda, *Cartes* 40).

From the beginning of the correspondence the inability to write, sometimes prompted directly by her love for Obiols, sometimes indirectly, is mentioned over and over. During the episode of his wife's trip to France she writes, "I neither write nor do anything...All of me is a burning hell" (Rodoreda, *Cartes* 81). Often she is simply too tired to write, because she has to make a living for the two of them:

> Since the Germans left...and I feel somewhat safe, I have got the writing bug. The tragedy is that I cannot write. I work myself into a stupor to earn a miserable living. I make nightgowns and slips for a luxury boutique. I must say I do it masterfully (Rodoreda, *Cartes* 59).

Still, even in her blackest moments and during her most unproductive periods, Rodoreda never forgets that she is a writer. The very process of writing is therapeutic. One of her early letters, which begins with a heartrending account of her miseries, makes an about-turn in the middle: "Writing, writing, Madam has calmed down a bit, Madam has regained her composure..." (Rodoreda, *Cartes* 42) and she goes on to recount with unabashed enthusiasm her plans for finishing the play that she is working on, and having it translated and performed in France.

The most striking element in these letters, however, is the drastic change in tone whenever she talks about her writing prospects. The whimpering masochist becomes as self-assured as if she had already achieved her place as Catalonia's foremost writer. Furthermore, she shows a remarkable willingness to adapt her writing to her circumstances. Spending endless hours at her sewing, she cannot muster the time, the energy or the concentration to write a novel. Instead, she makes out a master plan for a collection of fifty short stories, a three-year protect which she begins by systematically reading Steinbeck, Hemingway, Dorothy Parker and her favorite, Katherine Mansfield. "I plan to write stories that will make God tremble," she proclaims between nightgowns in 1946 (Rodoreda, *Cartes* 70).

One particular letter, also written in Bordeaux, radiates will power and self-assurance:

...what I will not leave behind in France is my energy or my youth.... You'll hear from me yet. And, above all, I want to write, I need to write. Nothing has given me as much pleasure, in my entire life, as a newly printed book of mine, with the smell of fresh ink still on its pages. ...I regret all these useless, demoralizing years, but I'll get even. I will make them useful, stimulating, so that my enemies will tremble. At the first chance I'll make a grand entrance. No one will be able to stop me (Rodoreda, *Cartes* 66).

As it happened, no one could. In 1954 she and Obiols went to live in Geneva, and in 1957 her collection of stories, *Vintidós contes*, several of which were first sketched in her letters, won the prestigious Víctor Català prize. Her trips to Barcelona became more frequent, and so did her publications and the acclaim that greeted her. She and Obiols never married, and one wonders if she continued to care that they didn't. When she settled back in Catalonia she was a mythical figure, not only the grande dame of Catalan letters but a living testimonial that not even exile could smother the Catalan flame, that thirty years of repression could not kill Catalonia's language or its genius.

Anna Murià returned to Catalonia with Bartra in 1970. Hers was not a grand entrance, although her husband was received with considerable fanfare. She who almost 50 years ago blissfully became the extension of her man continues to live quietly, and is hardly mentioned in Catalan literary circles.

In a letter dated shortly after Murià's departure, Rodoreda writes to her friend, "Love has maimed you, I hope Bartra will forgive me for saying this." In the letter which was returned from France Murià responds, "Ai, Mercè, I think you are more maimed than I" (Rodoreda, *Cartes* 51). In different ways, both Rodoreda and Murià were maimed by love, and their reciprocal diagnoses stand as tragic confirmation of how rarely love, fulfilled or unfulfilled, works as a positive force in a woman's life.

Fund for the Improvement
of Postsecondary Education
Office of Education
Washington, D.C. 20208

Works Cited

Burbano, Luis. "Mercedes Rodoreda, 'Premi Creixells,'" *La Vanguardia española* (31 de diciembre de 1937).

Folch i Pi, Núria. "Pròleg," in Rodoreda, Mercè, *La mort i la primavera*. Barcelona: Club Editor, 1986.

La Rochefoucauld. "Maximes," in Bishop, Morris, *A Survey of French Literature*. New York: Harcourt, Brace and World, 1955. Vol. I.

Murià, Anna. *L'obra de Bartra*. Barcelona: Vosgos, 1975.

Rodoreda, Mercè. *Cartes a l'Anna Murià, 1939-1956*. Barcelona: La Sal, 1985.

Woolf, Virginia. *A Room of One's Own*. New York: Harcourt, Brace and World, 1929.

Patricia J. Boehne

"ÉS QUAN DORMO QUE HI VEIG CLAR" (CATALAN POETRY FROM 1950 TO THE FUTURE)

It is a pleasure to share with you some ideas on contemporary Catalan poetry—where it has been and where it is going. I would like to begin with a poem of J.V. Foix, whose centennial year is coming to a close. He has been honored and remembered in this country, in Barcelona and around the world during 1993. I remember him with reverence and deep affection. Foix influenced many writers who have come after him, and in particular they responded to this poem from his 1953 volume *On he deixat les claus....* Some felt at the time of its publication that Foix was making a political statement, but then and through the years he insisted that it was not political or imitative of anyone. It refers to his own poetic process of "dreaming" poems and rising from his bed at dawn to type them. In it he evokes the frenzy, essence and aesthetic joy of the poet at the moment of creation:

I'ts when sleeping that I see clearly[1]
'Tis when it rains that I dance alone
Clothed in algae, gold and scales,
There is a scrap of tossing sea
And a shred of scarlet sky,
A bird circles above
And a mata trails its branches,
The pirate's hideout

Is a broad sun-flower.
'tis when it rains that I dance alone
Clothed in algae, gold and scales.
'Tis when I laugh that I see I'm twisted
In the pond below the tares,
I garb myself as an ancient
And approach the farmer's wife,
and mid pines and oak
I plant my flag;
With a pack needle
I kill the unnameable monster.
'Tis when I laugh that I see I'm twisted
In the pond below the tares.
'Tis when sleeping that I see clearly
Maddened by a sweet poison,
with pearls in each hand
I live in the heart of a scallop,
I am the spring in the valley
And the lair of the wild beast
—Or the moon thinning out
As it dies beyond the ridge.
'Tis when sleeping that I see clearly
Maddened by a sweet poison.[2]

It seems that Catalan poetry at the present moment is in transition in form, style and direction. With the political stability provided in recent years and the memories of unhappy times becoming ever more distant, the acceptance of the language ever greater, another "new generation" is beginning to emerge.

In addition, this past decade has seen the death of several great poetic figures of Catalan poetry. Those noted poets still alive and read are falling silent, and with perhaps one or two exceptions are not attempting to cross new frontiers.

This study is a brief, personal and initial attempt to assess the scope of contemporary Catalan poetry from 1950 to the present, a very large task. There has been an impressive outpouring of poetry and prose during these 40+ years, and I will limit myself to chronological observations on some of the more prominent poets in six eclectic groupings, realizing that even as we gather today there are new voices appearing in all regions of Catalonia.

Scholars more timely and knowledgeable than I have written and are writing on this topic. For earlier poets one may consult Fuster, and up to 1985, *Història de la literatura catalana*, vol. 10, Riquer/Comas/Molas, as well as other works, reviews, and the poems themselves. In self-defense, I can only say that from this side of the Atlantic, far from the cafes, bookstores and poetry readings in Barcelona and Valencia, one evaluates and studies the poems alone on the black and white page, attempting a dispassionate, distant view. The study of current Catalan poetry in North America is quite limited, in fact, as is its present popularity among our colleagues. For some time in our professional meetings I have not observed a presentation on the more youthful poets. There was a phase of interest in the "nova cançó" in the late 1970s and early 1980s. At the recent Seventh Col·loqui of NACS in Berkeley there were only five papers presented on Catalan poets from over 100 speakers. These were on Foix, Espriu, Verdaguer, and one contemporary Valencian poet, Josep Piera, born in 1947.

Among the longer dead poets most often cited by the younger contemporary writers are Salvat-Papasseit, Gabriel Ferrater, Carles Riba, Josep Carner, Rosselló-Pòrcel and J.V. Foix, who continued to publish, influence and mentor until his death in 1987. Foix and Salvador Espriu, who died in 1985, both continued to publish major works until their deaths. They will certainly stand as two of the greatest Catalan poets of the 20th century. Among those joining them in death were Agustí Bartra, writing in Catalan and Spanish from Mexico, Joan Vinyoli, Joan Oliver,

known as the ironic Pere Quart, Joan Fuster, Gabriel Ferrater, Marià
Manent and recently Vicent André Estellès from Valencia. Joan Brossa
and Màrius Torres should be included in listing the poets of this period.
Each of these aforementioned poets is highly individualistic; one cannot
speak of them as a "generation" except in terms of birth chronology and
the shared experiences of the war and its aftermath. In a 1985 conversation with Narcís Comadira, Foix referred to generational groupings as
10-year categories. He felt that he shared a birth generation with Carles
Riba and López-Picó, but not with Josep Carner, whose own birth
generation was preceded by Bofill i Mates. In fact, critics all agree that
only the earliest work of Foix, such as visual poetry, can be classified
as part of any movement. He defies all generational labels.

The deaths of these poets during the past few years leaves a major
void in Catalan letters. However, some poets who are older now are still
producing work into their later years. Among these are J. M. Llompart
of Mallorca, a member of the 1950's Generation of Mallorcan poets,
Martí i Pol, born 1929 and especially active during the 1970s and 1980s,
Blai Bonet, Villangómez Llobet, and other writers in Catalunya Nord and
Alguer. For the most part this 2nd group is writing reflective summa-
tions of poetic life. Tomàs Garcés, for example, published with
regularity from 1931 to 1955. *Plec de Poemes* appeared in 1971 and
Escrit a terra in 1985, late for his generation.

In addition to Catalan poets writing in Catalan, there are today
Gatalans writing poetry in Castilian who have earned renown. Our friend
Manuel Duran, similar to Bartra, was an exile in Mexico. In addition to
his Castilian poems, he now writes lyric poetry in Catalan. Enric Badosa,
close to Foix, translates Catalan poetry to Castilian and laments that he
writes his own works in Castilian as well. Gimferrer was able to make
the linguistic transition to Catalan.

Among the younger group of already recognized poets are Pere

Gimferrer, born 1945, Marta Pessarrodona, born 1941, Francesc Par-
cerisas, born 1944, Josep Piera of Valencia, born 1947 and Narcís
Comadira, born 1942. Some of them are at times referred to as the
Generation of the 70s.

They have written at a time of political transition. Gimferrer,
heavily influenced by Foix, has been doing a great deal of prose writing
and criticism in recent years. His first volume, *Els Miralls,* appeared in
1970. That was his most fertile decade. Parcerisas, born 1944, has
published three major works, *Vint poemes civils*, 1961, *Latitud dels
cavalls,* 1974, and *L'Edat d'or*, 1933. He has been influenced by visual,
musical and European authors. number of the younger poets, male and
female, make reference by name in their poems to European sources
such as poets, novelists and places. They have ventured beyond
Catalonia, are reading widely, and choosing European cultural models
as sources of inspiration. There inspiration is from without, and at that,
from outside Catalonia. This is a bit disconcerting to traditionalists and
seekers of "pure poetry."

Marta Pessarrodona's poems are collected in a volume ranging
from 1969-81. Her fascination with Germany and her love affair with
Gabriel Ferrater as well as her feminine persona are major features of
her writings.

Narcís Comadira, whose work is largely collected in a 1970-1980
volume, is also a member of this chronological group. He is a personal
writer, self-directed, as is each one of this grouping.

Alex Susanna, who was a surrealist until the 1980s, has published
Abandonadament, 1977, and *Les anelles dels anys*, 1990. The latter is
more precise and controlled. Its themes are time and love, also used by
Gimferrer.

The poems of Josep Piera, another poet of the 1970s, according
to J. M. Sala-Valldaura, are filled with "new Mediterraneanism" in his

notable volume *Maremar*, intimate and sensual in contemplation. Piera has been referred to by others as part of "la segona ona de la Generació dels 70."

Between this grouping and the present is a transitional and yet traditional writer, Albert Ràfols-Casamada. Time is a major theme. His important work began to appear between 1979 and 1989, in such volumes as *Territori de temps, Angle de llum* and *El color de les pedres*. Early on, influences of Baudelaire, Verlaine and Foix are apparent. There is a continuous preoccupation with time, existence, Catalan being, and what some have called the "anxiety" or "angst" of the Mediterranean man. Foix's own anxiety concerning time and being stem from Henri Bergson. Ràfols-Casamada continues in this vein. Ràfols-Casamada is writing and publishing at a time of fascinating transition, from the late 1970s through the 1980s, a time when Catalonian language and culture are affirming their identity and at the same time discarding old models and searching for new voices. It is a time in which poets ask themselves "How should I write? Whom should I look to? Should I become European? Global? Neoclassic?"

Ràfols-Casamada has chosen a moderate, classic course. He accepts his identity as a Catalan poet in the following ways: His vocabulary is pure, classical Catalan and yet homey, domestic at times; his love of Catalan paisatge and nature are nearly always present. His "Mediterranean anxiety" which is concerned with time, memory and being reflects itself in a yearning for roots and a questing for future Catalan reality after 1975. In "Roc mestral" there is a concreteness of reality in his assessment of abstract time. The poem is written as a cantata, with overture, duets, arias and chorus. Here is the closing chorus from "Roc mestral," 1979, translated by Sam Abrams, in which he combines memory and future. I believe it is representative of the sensibilities of this generation and may stand the test of time:

(chorus)

we notice with the yellow
of lemons
the outline of things

skipping suddenly
from desire to memory
like knives or lips

time to remember
glass crevices
in the damp sand wall

time to doubt
interwoven paths
under rain

iron mirror
the opaque sea outstretches
waiting is torn

a rainbow
raises its arm
over flat-roofs and chimneys

where will we find what we were
in what we are?
space that shatters day by day?

time to remember
time for expectation
where are the smoke and wine and laughter?

where are the green grapes
afternoons of sleeping clocks
joyful hands?

open balcony braids

wings of burning looks
lavender embraces

time to remember
time to doubt
stubble and level grass

that hand writing
eyes watching
the landscape lost in the storm

trees and trails
the song of the hoopoo
the flight of partridges and magpies

the smoldering city
at the foot of kisses
all the gardens of colors and words

all things are the precise moment
transparence and echo
the moment the leaf falls[3]

Another poem by Ràfols-Casamada, "L'ombra dels núvols," written in 1989, is dedicated to his parents. It utilizes the passing of a generation and generations as a testimony to change, the future, and yet to memory of past beauty:

What slope did time roll down?
darkness and light like weightless water
slide over an initial body
darkness and light rolling down the slope to the river
tender body the voices accompany you like Ariadne's
thread down the path and into time

there is no valid protest
nor corners to hide this landscape's grief

ruthless mirror where lost smiles
wage war on helpless tears

there is no possible protest or refusal
in such a large space where absences sail
evening light dim radiance
white clouds on the canvas
over the distant forest where chiseled forms
waver as if the wind driving distance
were trying to tie them all in one bunch
a bird probably flew by

and the dog suddenly threw barks into the air
suspecting someone was perhaps coming close
on the path that in the painting is lost behind the bushes
that a precise stroke of the brush and the hand define[4]

While it may not be politically correct, I have chosen to group most of the women poets together. Their themes often deal with love and a personal viewpoint. However, advancing chronologically, one finds that women poets can certainly choose and articulate the same topics as male poets.

Both Clementina Arderiu, born 1889 and Rosa Leveroni, born 1910 were students of Carles Riba. Riba was Arderiu's husband as well. Arderiu's *Obra poètica* appeared in 1973, Leveroni's *Poesia* in 1981. Both women lived long enough and at the apex of Catalan culture and poetry to produce memorable work. Their presence dominated feminine writing well beyond their productive years.

Later women authors seem to gravitate toward other genres, poetry being only one of several. Representative are Maria Àngels Anglada, born 1930. Her poetic works, largely based on Greek and Latin classics, are collected in a 1990 volume, *Columnes d'hores*. Olga Xirinacs the novelist, born 1936, is also a poet, noted for her musicality.

Her poetic publication commences in 1977. Her 1990 volume is *La pluja sobre els palaus*.

Marta Pessarrodona, born in 1941 would logically be discussed next chronologically. For her choice of themes and influences I have placed her with the writers of the 1970s. Her collection, *Poesia*, appeared in 1984. Since then, German culture and ethos have redirected her writing. Maria-Mercè Marçal, born 1952, is a strong, feminist voice writing with a rebellion unlike most of the Catalan poets of this century. She is vehemently searching out her personal identity. Such a search may prove to have been an intuitive metaphor fifty years from now. Her poetry from 1973-88 has been collected in *Llengua abolida*, 1989.

Just as there are many male poets who should be mentioned in a longer and less eclectic study, there is a substantial number of women poets who deserve more than a brief mention. Among the 60 Catalan women writers highlighted by the Institució de les Lletres Catalanes, 29 are poets, and many write in multiple genres. A bilingual, chronological sampling of Catalan women poets was published with English translations by Sam Abrams in 1991 entitled *Survivors*. It includes Ma. Antònia Salvà, Arderiu, Leveroni, Montserrat Abelló, Felicià Fuster, Ma. Àngels Anglada, Pessarrodona, Margarita Ballester and Maria-Mercè Marçal.

The sixth group to be mentioned is the newest generation, those born between 1956 and 1970 and who began to publish in the mid-1980s. Their work is award-winning, but they have yet to stand the test of time. Their poetry seems to have escaped the influences of their most immediate predecessors, and yet these have enriched the youngest voices. Perhaps the styles employed by these youthful poets is what marks them as strikingly different. They have grown up in a radically different time than that of contemporary poets mentioned earlier or even Martí i Pol, for example, whose popular *Estimada Marta* was published in 1978. Sala-Valldaura has a rather harsh critique of the poetry of the 1980s. He feels they are certainly not a poetic generation, nor is their inspiration original or classic. My impression is that he feels Catalan poetry is in the trough of a wave, not a crest.

In these times poets and scholars have access to the complete published works of poets as recent as Salvador Espriu, J.V. Foix, Marià Manent, Vicent Andrés Estellès, all dying in 1985 or later. These have no doubt been read or at least consulted by the youngest new poets. Any influence stemming from these "recent classics," however, is presently unclear. Let us recall, also, that all publication in Catalan is far easier and less selective than it was for the poets named above, who wrote in secret, and in difficult times. We may never see their early efforts, unlike the youthful poets of today. These circumstances cloud our efforts to fully understand and appreciate some of the current poetic output.

For example, a volume such as *Per Puck*, 1992 by Feliu Formosa is highly unusual and significant. It contains 28 sections describing theater as art in prose poems and poetry. It is not only difficult to classify; it also fits no earlier category clearly. Like Ràfols-Casamada's "cantata," Formosa is creating a new form. The content, however, is removed from Catalan reality into the abstract world of art, perhaps a reaction which was inevitable. 1986 marked the centenary of Verdaguer's *Canigó*, which may have contributed to a reaction against "purely catalan" content. Formosa's 1986 *Semblança* is more traditional. It presents 16 love poems more in the vein of Pedro Salinas.

A seminal volume for studying the youngest poets, those of the post-1970s generation, is a 1989 anthology *Ser del segle, Antologia de nous poetes catalans*. Among those published in this anthology are various prize winners, all born after 1956 and as late as 1966. Their consciousness has a radically different formation. Their writing is a clear departure from Catalan writing of the 20th century. They feel freer thematically than Catalan poets have felt for centuries; they are unfettered by the former weight of language and culture.

A sampling of these poets will include: Montserrat Llorens, Antoni Tàpies-Barba, born 1956, who published *Matèria dels astres* in 1992. He is concerned with style. Ramon Guillem, born 1959, is concerned with style as formal perfection. A writer of poetry and prose, he published *Les ombres seduïdes* in 1991. Carles Torner, born 1963, is a humanist who is concerned with the magical and the spiritual. He has published *La ciutat blanca*, 1984, *Als límits de la sal*, 1985 and *L'àngel del saqueig*, 1991. Vicenç Llorca, born 1965, is influenced by the classics. He has authored *L'amic desert,* 1991.

Others are Margalida Pons, born 1966, author of *Les aus*, 1988, Josep Ballester, noted for his original use of language with *Oasi*, 1989, Antoni Puig-Verd, a formalist, with *Curset de natació*, 1991, and winner of the Carles Riba prize, and Gabriel Planella, *Roda*, 1992, with a strong interest in nature.

Salvador Espriu published *Cementiri de Sinera* in 1946, and perhaps we should date contemporary Catalan poetry from its appearance as a great and original work. J. M. Castellet feels that it may not yet be completely comprehended, but that it is a milestone in the post-war development of Catalan poetry. It is thoroughly Catalan in spirit and locus, metaphysical in its treatment of death and memory. These themes and the segmented structure are taken up by some later poets.

Some of the most important works are clustered around 1960-65, which seems to be a seminal time for appreciating Catalan poetry of the second half of the 20th century. Carles Riba had died in 1959, ending an era. Other influential writers became widely known and available. Espriu's *La pell de brau* burst into public view in 1960. (Foix's *El pell de la pell* illustrated by Ponç came out in 1974.) Gabriel Ferrater published *Da nuces pueris* that year. Pere Quart's *Vacances pagades* first appeared in 1960. Foix published *Onze nadals i un cap d'any* in 1960 and his *Obres poètiques* in 1964, which gathered most of his earlier and inaccessible writings. This work became important for a broad understanding of Foix, and the volumes and editions which followed gave him wide readership in all circles. His complete works began appearing in 1974. Among the oldest members of the groups we have seen today, Marià Manent published *La ciutat del temps* in 1961, his last book of verse and the only one since *L'ombra i altres poemes* in 1931. The complete works of Carles Riba were not published until 1965-67. This last date reminds one of the discontinuity of tradition for young poets. They lacked sources to gain a full panorama of 20th century Catalan poetry. Much of the poetry to which they did have access was from French, German and English sources.

At present as the century closes, young authors seem more concerned with form than content. Are they neoclassic? It is a reaction, while abrupt, which might have been expected. While the burden of their language and culture is lessened, the artistic search for an authentic voice may be even more arduous. Time and readership will show whether this group can fill the places left by the departed voices of the 20th century.

Dept. of Foreign Languages
Eastern College
St. David's, PA 19087

ENDNOTES

[1] Original title: "On he deixat les claus...." From: "Selection of Foix's Poems." *Catalan Review* 1 (june, 1986). Transl. by Patricia Boehne.

[2] Cat.: És quan plou que ballo sol / Vestit d'algues, or i escata, / Hi ha un pany de mar al revolt / I un tros de cel escarlata, / Un ocell fa un giravolt / I treu branques una mata, / El casalot del pirata / És un ample gira-sol. / És quan plou que ballo sol / Vestit d'algues, or i

escata. // És quan ric que em veig gepic / Al bassal de sota l'era, / Em vesteixo d'home antic / I empaito la masovera, / I entre pineda i garric / Planto la meva bandera; / Amb una agulla saquera / Mato el monstre que no dic. / És quan ric que em veig gepic / Al bassal de sota l'era. // És quan dormo que hi veig clar / Foll d'una dolça metzina, / Amb perles a cada mà / Visc al cor d'una petxina, / Só la font del comellar / I el jaç de la salvatgina, / —O la lluna que s'afina / En morir carena enllà. / És quan dormo que hi veig clar / Foll d'una dolç metzina. Abril de 1939.

[3] Cat.: (cor) // remarquem amb el groc / de les llimones / el perfil de les coses // saltar de sobte / entre anhel i memòria / com ganivets o llavis//temps de record / escletxes de cristall / al mur de sorra humida // temps de dubte / camins entrelligats / sota la pluja //mirall de plom / s'estira el mar opac / s'esquincen les esperes // un arc de sant martí / aixeca el braç / per damunt de terrats i xemeneies // on trobarem el que érem / dins el que som? / l'espai que s'esmicola dia a dia? // temps de record / temps d'aguait / on són el fum i el vi i les rialles? // on són el raïm verd / les tardes de rellotge adormit / les mans alegres? // trenes de balcó obert / ales d'esguards encesos / abraçades d'espígol // temps de record / temps de dubte / rostolls i herba rasa // aquella mà que escriu / els ulls que observen / el paisatge perdut en la tempesta // els arbres i els corriols / el cant de la puput / el vol de la perdiu i de la garsa // la ciutat fumejant / al peu de les besades / tots els jardins de colors i paraules // tot és l'instant precís / transparència i ressò / l'instant de la fulla quan cau.

[4] Cat.: Quin pendent el temps ha corregut? // ombra i llum com una aigua lleugera / llisquen damunt un cos inicial / ombra i llum rodolant pendent avall fins al riu / tendre cos t'acompanyen les veus com un fil / d'Ariadna camí enllà i temps endins // no hi ha protesta vàlida / ni racons on amagar el dolor d'aquest paisatge / mirall inclement on somriures perduts / enceten el combat amb indefenses llàgrimes // no hi ha protesta ni refús possibles/dins un espai tan gran on absències naveguen // llum de capvespre resplendor esmorteïda / núvols blancs damunt la tela / damunt el bosc llunyà on formes escarpades / oscil·len com si el vent empenyent les distàncies / volgués lligar-les totes en un sol ramell / algun ocell segurament volava // i el gos de cop llançà lladrucs a l'aire / sospitant que potser algú s'apropava / pel camí que al quadre es perd rere les mates / que un toc precís de pinzell i la mà defineixen.

Enric Bou

"SILENCI EN UN JARDÍ":
MÀRIUS TORRES
AND THE CATALAN LITERARY TRADITION

Màrius Torres was a poet of extraordinary secrecy. One of the last writers whose work was not published during his lifetime. Maybe because of this, maybe because of other reasons, a significant devotion towards his work and life has developed in Catalonia after his death in 1942. I was in Lleida about a year ago where I witnessed the degree of this devotion. At the Ateneu Popular de Ponent the City Hall had very carefully organized a well-rounded exhibition about his life and times, which included a reproduction of his room at the sanitarium in Puig d'Olena, where he died. The organizers, mainly Margarida Prats, had carefully chosen items from his manuscripts and his private library which had been carefully kept by Núria and Víctor, his brother and sister. A few months later, last May, I was able to observe how Núria Torres and Margarida Prats were adding the final touches to a slimmer version of the same exhibition that was about to open at the Main Hall of the University of Barcelona, an honor that only a few writers have shared with him. At that time I asked myself "what are the reasons for this kind of interest, or perhaps devotion?" I would like to share with you this morning some of the answers I have musing over since those days.

First, we could give some "local" explanation. Tip O'Neil once said that world politics always start at the local level, and the same could be said of poetry. If an author thrills his or her neighborhood, he or she has already gained the most fervent of his or her readers. And this, indeed, happened to Màrius Torres, because his love for his home city of Lleida is evident in more than one verse. And not only that: his is a love that transmutes and renames the relationship between a community and its entourage. Therefore, in many of his verses there occurs that magical identification between a community and some ideas expressed through poetry which people feel to be representative of their own past or present way of living. This is the case of popular poetry, and also of some Catalan writers such as Jacint Verdaguer, Joan Maragall and Josep M. de Sagarra. Think only of such well known "songs" as "L'emigrant," "L'Empordà," "Vinyes verdes vora el mar," "La fira de Santa Llúcia"—or the voices of Emili Vendrell, Lluís Llach. These are well known texts by lesser known authors, although they are well established "high-cult" writers.

In Torres' poem "Molt lluny d'aquí," we read:[1]

Sé una ciutat, molt lluny d'aquí, dolça i secreta,
on els anys d'alegria són breus com una nit;
on el sol és feliç, el vent és un poeta,
i la boira és fidel com el meu esperit

Only those who have endured, and even enjoyed Lleida's mythical "boira" (fog) can truly understand the subtle irony that blends with affect imbedded in these verses, and how, in the end, hides a profound love for a particular place.

Beyond what we may call the "local" level, Màrius Torres "grandeur" is definitely related to two opposite reasons: his critical imbrication in the Catalan literary tradition; and the opening of new ventures for that same tradition. What is most specific about Torres literary work? What are the main differences (and similarities) between his poetry and that of other writers of his time? Does his geographical origin play any significant role? Was the diffusion (and reception) of his work tainted by the time when it happened, during Franco's dictatorship?

These are some of the urgent questions that critics still have to answer about Màrius Torres poetry. I will not be able, of course, to answer all of them today, only a few, but I believe those questions led us to a certain path which we may follow in order to read Torres against the poetry of his time.

Joan Sales was Màrius Torres closest friend and the one responsible for us being here. He exchanged a correspondence with Torres, which included his poetry and he finally published it in Mexico, in 1947.[2] Sales put a lot of effort into this relationship (a similar one to that developed later on with Mercè Rodoreda). He helped Torres with many comments and corrections, and he was the first one to note his singularity. In a letter from 9 July 1938 he wrote:[3]

> Amb la teva nova "manera," a partir del *Dolç Angel de la Mort,* t'apartes de la de tots els que a Catalunya i en aquest segle t'han precedit en l'ús de la paraula—entre els quals n'hi ha alguns de tan il·lustres i molts de tan benemèrits—; te n'apartes, no solament per l'estil i pel llenguatge, sinó sobretot per l'esperit. La teva poesia és tan "lírica" i ho és tan exclusivament que quan n'intentes d'una altra mena, narrativa, o descriptiva, fracasses; "líric" vol dir subjectiu, personal, introvertit, o no vol dir res. Els teus millors moments són precisament els que més s'assemblen a una "confession de minuit." A Catalunya i en el nostre segle només n'hi ha hagut una altra que ho fos tant, la de Salvat-Papasseit, tan ignorat pels nostres sapientíssims crítics; pero només a llampecs fugaços. ...és el cas que la poesia de tots ells [els bons poetes catalans del segle XX], amb la sola excepció del millors moments de Salvat-Papasseit, és més aviat descriptiva, narrativa, decorativa, patriòtica o humorística i sembla més un exercici literari que no pas una "confession de minuit."
>
> (364-365)

Sales' words are very important because help us to focus on the core of Torres' work. That is his centrality in Catalan poetry of mid Twentieth century. A centrality hidden by the harsh conditions of the early diffusion of his work, but that in the end have accomplished a secret wish of Torres himself: to be read in another century.

Although Màrius Torres lived a short life he had time to construct a very solid work. He has been most fortunate in terms of the critical attention devoted to his work: several biographies, six editions which include letters and other documents, and many articles. Jordi Pàmies, a fellow poet and "lleidatà" has indicated four themes: beauty of the world, night, death and God. Pere Gimferrer noted Torres devotion towards his dedication "en l'entorn immediat—els cicles de la naturalesa—i en els problemes fonamentals de la condició de l'home i el seu destí metafísic i la capacitat de l'art per expressar-los" (11). Gimferrer, like Sales, stressed the condition of Torres of being eccentric in European poetry of the 1930's, because his strong debt towards Baudelaire.

We realize that critics agree in noting Torres' attraction towards Symbolism. It could be also added that his correspondence with Carles Riba, during the last months of his life, has helped to create the image of a writer attracted by "pure poetry." His debts with Symbolism were noted also by Sales:[4]

> Hi ha un cert gènere "molt Màrius" en què les estrofes, alternant alexandrins i versos d'altres mesures, són d'una música alada i melangiosa que expressa admirablement els estats d'esperit més difícils de dir (366).

Indeed, this portray of a "gènere 'molt Màrius'" is very similar to that of post-symbolist poetry written by C. M. Bowra. He talked of poets who:

...attempted to convey a supernatural experience in the language of visible things, and therefore almost every word is a symbol and is used not for its common purpose but for the association which it evokes of a reality beyond the senses (5).

Post-symbolist writers are (in)famous for their willingness to communicate a supernatural experience with words that belong to everyday vocabulary. The use of symbolic constructions may express this reality not seen. There has always been much discussion about their connection with reality. Torres is not an exception: critics have developed his image of a writer with an extremely rich inner life who writes about the real world almost by accident. But are we being fair with him? I do not think so. His is a poetry that compared with other writers of his time abounds in references to the real world. In a letter to Joan Sales stated his commitment: "Our times," reads a letter from January 1942, "marks such a dizzying descent of civilization that many times Europeans feel an emptiness in our stomachs, like that when one goes down in an elevator too quickly" (245). Or in another: "Notre époque sera pour longtemps une inconnue. Nous avons assisté à ses premiers gestes ~ nous avons saisi sa grandeur. mais nous ignorons tout de ses secrètes pensées" (220).

Torres is original because he was able to combine two literary traditions: a militant one, devoted to make revolution triumph; and that of the followers of Symbolism, with a much more metaphysical approach and arcane vocabulary. At the heart of his poetry we can confirm an obsession with symbolist topics and rhythms. Think of fire, poetry and the poet, an irreconcilable passion for absolute. Or such elements as rose, garden, secret city. Màrius Torres had the idea that he was witness to a terrible upheaval in civilization. And this, indeed, had an impact in his "Weltanschauung." In his case the world's malaise has another correlative in his own situation, separated from the world because of his

tuberculosis. The confluence of both situations helped him a lot in order
to establish a refuge through poetry. His extreme solitude helped him to
develop this new kind of poetry made out of the combination of
introspection and atterition towards collective feelings.

The work alone of a specific writer—when it is a good one—
produces very characteristic illuminations. It is like a map of passion and
diction, a way of self delivery in front of the reader. When the same
work is compared to a whole period we receive new illuminations that
tinge our first impression. This is why, following in part Sales advice in
the first letter I quoted, I want to explain the use of a specific topics as
is the Garden.

When referring to gardens in literature we may say what Oscar
Wilde once said about people who love to talk about the weather: they
always mean something else. The same thing happens to gardens. As
stated by Robert Harbison: "Every garden is a replica, a representation,
an attempt to recapture something, but the form it finds for the act is that
of a mental picture, so in spite of its special properties a garden is just
another of the images of art" (3).

In fact Catalan poets only adopt a long-standing European and
local tradition. This a symbolic space that in its origin relates to
"Paradise," and has always the added value of acting as a refuge or
defense against the inconveniences from life.

As Simon Pugh has written:

> The garden is a pervasive metaphor in culture (not just of the
> west). The metaphoric reference point of gardens is the idea of
> the garden as paradise, the site of travesty, a falling away from
> bliss, but also the site of childhood, of both precultural bliss and
> of acculturation. As a lost state that is recreated trough represen-
> tation, the garden is the site of desire (Pugh, 2).

In late Nineteenth century and early Twentieth century the garden has a meaning as a space where wilderness or free nature merges with human control, and may remind us of a happier time when there was a much clear separation between nature and city.

A garden has elements inherited from the *locus amoenus*: a tree or a small forest, a fountain, a meadow to lie down and rest. From Fray Luis de León to San Juan de la Cruz; from Verdaguer who made his characters rest in the "Garden of the Hespèrides" to Joan Maragall enchanted by the Pirynees. A *locus amoenus* represented a place for happiness, small version of paradise, with a stopped time, where human beings can be happy without any restraints. In fact, this is the place where there is an integration between, wild nature and civilization.

If we focus on Catalan poetry from Modernisme onward we can define two types of garden. One is the garden as a setting, a place for profound meditation. The other is a garden presented as a smaller version of a general landscape. In both cases the garden is used to express a more complex thought or reality.

In Catalan Modernisme the garden became emblematic of several things. Santiago Rusiñol presented a summary of his thought on this matter in speeches such as the one delivered at the 1894 "Tercera festa modernista" in Sitges. There he expressed a very productive symbolic association: "Tot pels horts productius d'una prosa alimentícia i estragada, i res pels jardins de l'ànima, pels florits caminals de la poesia!" This rather elemental image was useful to express the opposition between poetry and prose, between material and soul. At any rate we are still very far from Màrius Torres exquisite presentation of similar problems.

Santiago Rusiñol main interest on gardens was related to the capacity which he discovered in them of concentrating exquisite sensations, and of substantiate an artistic experience. The importance of the garden in his work can also be noticed by his recurrence both in literature and painting. In one of the prose poems in *Oracions* (1897) he established with acute exactitude the deep meaning of gardens in his personal poetics. In "An els jardins abandonats," gardens are presented as places where wild nature fights the influence of human beings. Therefore they are associated with a better past, as some kind of museum constructed out of "essència de paisatge." Finally he also considered them to be beauty's graveyard. The basic idea is that gardens are "ruïnes vives i oasis de poesia." In another prose of the same book we can read: "No despertis el seu son, no moguis ni profanis aquelles adormides cendres, no restauris aquelles pedres caigudes, que la Bellesa hi arrela i es nodreix dels records que l'assaonen, i les ruïnes són llibres vells i complerts, amb l'última plana escrita."[5] This coincides with some of the metaphors—two delicate places, garden and ruin as symbol for his art—that we may locate in three of his 1898 paintings, "Palau abandonat," "El jardí abandonat" i "Caminal de rosers." We see images that send us back to some of the notes on his plays:[6]

> L'escena representa un jardí descuidat, un jardí clàssic, amb plantes nobles, emmalaltides pel descuit, i conservant el segell distingit que no tenen els jardins improvisats, un jardí amb pàtina de vellesa, modelat pels besos del temps i impregnat de la tristesa que donen els arbres antics i les plantes arrelades. A un costat, una glorieta de xiprers retallats amb simetria; al fons una graderia de marbre pintada per la molsa i amb les lloses esgrogueïdes; a la dreta, el palau, amb figures esgrafiades mig destenyides per la pluja; desmais i xiprers al lluny; en primer terme, un sortidor d'aigües quietes i somortes.

Again, the garden represents Art, melancholic Decadentism with aesthetical purpose. This may still be a simplistic version of Symbolism.

Other writers insisted in the garden motif. There the garden becomes a microcosmos, in a "plein air" situation, nature is under control. Joan Maragall in a well known poem in *Poesies*, from the series "Pirenenques" presents himself in the act of contemplating nature. A significant shift is the pantheist identification that the poet presents. In poem m we can read:[7]

> Ben ajagut a terra, com me plau
> el veure davant meu en costa suau
> un prat ben verd sota d'un cel ben blau!
> I en les albes la gran bellugadissa
> de les fulles d'acer que el vent eriça
> amb tants reflects de llum enlluernadissa.
>
> I el sol estès pertot.
>   I el rec com cau
> escumejant avall la costa suau
> del prat ben verd sota del cel ben blau.
> Tots els membres caiguts, tot jo per terra,
> buidat de tota ma força i sens desig,
> la pensa a poc a poc se'm desaferra...
> I em vaig trobant tan bé an allà entremig,
> i em va invadint com una immensa pau,
> i vaig sent un tros més del prat suau
> ben verd, ben verd sota d'un cel ben blau.

I mentioned before the fact that many gardens were conceived as a piece of a larger landscape using *locus amoenus elements*. In Maragall's case we may mention the tress, the river, the meadow, the blue sky, etc. Moreover, it is remarkable the fact that he includes his version of the garden in the middle of a well known mountain.

In the poetry of Josep Carner we witness other important changes. The garden is a correlative for religious devotions, in "El jardí desembral," because the garden is the "pessebre" dedicated to "Mare de Déu del Pi." Or in another instance, in "Aquesta fou la casa," the garden acts as mute witness to the happy time of adolescence and the first when he is 15 years old:

> Vinc sol avui, en matinada freda.
> Veig el verger, la font i la pineda
> plena dels murmuris musicals d'ahir,
>   i encara, sota del brancal, m'espia
> la dolça por del temps de primeria
> que amb la mà alçada oprimeix el si.

Maybe the most innovative development appears in his well-known poem "Retorn a Catalunya." There we can detect a very sophisticated reelaboration of Maragall's appropriation of a segment of nature. Carner in turn presents a generic Catalan landscape as a garden:[8]

> Ja veig damunt la serra de foc el nostre pi.
> Oh gent que per les feixes daurades feu camí!
> Em sobta com un vi
> la força tota vella humil que ens agermana.
> (És viu com la ginesta i com el blau marí
> el teu escarafall, oh noia catalana.)
>   Com somrieu en hores del vespre, masos blancs,
> entre pallers de bona companyia,
> i cada mas ateny en curta rodalia
> bosquet i blat i vinya i un marge amb tres pollancs.
>   Voldria, tot perdent-me per valls i fondalades,
> dir tes llaors, oh terra de salut!,
> enmig de coses fosques i vides oblidades
> com aquest grill que canta dins un camí perdut.

This is a very impressive modification of the previous garden motif. It is much closer to the one we may encounter in post-symbolist writers. I find particularly interesting this conception of the whole country as a smaller *locus amoenus*. It is also remarkable that this is one of the first poems to propose a synthesis between a public and a private approach towards reality. But it is also worth noting that it includes an interesting similarity with a description that Torres made in a letter about the *Côte d'Azur:*[9]

> La Cote d'Azur no és un mite. Saint Raphael, el primer poble és una delícia. Muntanyoles suaus, de color d'aram a la vora, i blaves al fons, fan una cala ampla i profunda, com un gran riu aturat. Les cases són amples i vermelles amb horts de tarongers i geranis. Als llocs estratègics, una mica de verd, de pins (Prats, 37).

Even in a long poem from early 1937, dedicated to Mercè Figueres, Torres described the Vallès landscape surrounding Puig d'Olena, in a very similar manner:[10]

> Tu que estimes l'humil jardí de Puig d'Olena,
> on els arbres ardits es drecen a balquena
> entre el cel i la roca i la casa i el bosc.
> El jardí muntanyenc, senyorívol i tosc,
> Mercè, jo vull contar-te la seva primavera
> tímida, somrient, ingràvida, lleugera,
> que posa en el paisatge sever d'aquest país
> la gràcia positiva i tendra d'un somris.
> (...)
> Per sobre les carenes, verdes, blaves o grises
> altres terres s'eixamplen, ondulades o llises
> com l'amable Vallès, polit, familiar,
> que ple de fumeroles s'allarga fins al mar.
>
> (Torres 1978, 295-298)

I would like to end this review of the uses of the garden in Catalan poetry with a few examples from others poets who were active in Torres' time. Almost at random we may easily locate examples in the firsts books of poets such as Joan Vinyoli, Joan Teixidor or Bartomeu Rosselló-Porcel. Here are some valuable examples.

Critics have made a distinction between "dues elegies" in the poetry of Joan Vinyoli. The first one belongs to a "distensió il·lumina-da," and is related to a rural landscape, that of la Selva. The second one presents a desperate tone, in a screamful voice, where the poet talks about suburban landscapes. This is where the garden comes into being. In his first book, *Primer desenllaç* (1937), we find several poems located in gardens. Even the title of a whole section is precisely "Els jardins." In the first one, "A una estàtua en un jardí," the poet talks to an statue located in the middle of a blooming garden. There is a sharp contrast between the representation of a human being—a cold one—and the warm sight of Nature. The distance between them is stressed by an inanimate human being and flowers blooming. The garden alone, without any real human being in sight enacts the distance between both worlds. In other poems of the same series, "En un jardí," "Glorieta" i "Capvespre al jardí," Vinyoli insists in the idea of garden as secluded place—hortus conclusus—enacting concepts that are so dear to post-symbolist poets: the rose, night scenes, dreams.

In another example, in the poem suite "Aire d'elegia," a distant garden is the crucial setting related to the brief happiness of the lovers. It is also remarkable that the garden is already refereed to as "park" in his following book, *De vida i somni* (1948), and in the city it does not have any more that magical and mysterious aspect. He insists in an idea that we may also locate in Torres: the separation of worlds between garden and city.[11]

> El vespre apaga el crit innumerable
> metàl·lic, gris, de la ciutat i deixa
> sentir-se en l'ombra l'amorosa queixa
> dels atardats torbant l'impenetrable,
> melangiós interior: perduts
> són ara els límits, vagament perdura
> un so planyent entre les quietuds;
> alba de lluna als roserars fulgura.
>
>   ("El vell parc")

In later books by Vinyoli the city becomes a scenery with many and deep meanings. The garden is still important in "Estàtues en el jardí" from *Les hores retrobades* (1951), or "Un home al jardí" from *Realitats* (1963). As we know this last book begins a very different voice by Vinyoli, and precisely then the garden changes its meaning complete-ly:[12]

> Jo, ara, visc en el jardí quadrat
> d'un dia prou madur que ja no invoca
> fantasmes de passat ni de crepuscle.

In the poetry of Joan Teixidor, a poet with some debts to the Avant-garde, we locate another possibility:[13]

> Ai, ens separen carnins
> i prades sense herba verda,
> paisatge de maniquins
> i muntanyetes de cendra.

This is the poem "Lletra d'amor" in *Joc partit* (1935). In almost all the poems in this book Teixidor uses a similar setting for his lovers' world: fog, at either sunset or dawn, with some details of nature under control in the background. In the series "Elegia" the garden supplants the traditional one and is modified thanks to oneiric elements:[14]

> Record allunya aquelles tardes fines
> amb or guarnides, jovenívols passos
> pels llargs camins, pollancs, palmeres, aire,
> estany, ocells, crepuscle, vent, diàleg,
> font, àlber, banc—i la rotllana càndida
> de noies fràgils estremint-se certes,
> plenes de joc, sobtadament escàpoles.
>
> (III)

Màrius Torres condensed in a few motifs the core of his

message: "night," "roses," "river," "death," are some of the words which he uses most often, and that remind us about his plea for essenciatility, and his attempt to achieve victory against fugacity: "Mories poc a poc, i et tornaves, cantant, / una ombra que tenia la forma del teu cant." This is the complaint for the many difficulties when trying to understand reality, which appears to be a shadow of a song, death, etc. From his early compositions he is attracted by Garden and City.

Why does he insist in the garden? What is its meaning in Màrius Torres poetry? In the case of a poet like him when nobody has much trouble mentioning biographical facts in connection to the poems, there is an easy way out. The poet, we can say, persisted because it had a special meaning in his personal situation. Margarida Prats has explained it with close detail: at the sanitarium in Puig d'Olena patients alternated total calm and walks through the garden and visits to the library. It is worth noting that these two spaces are the only ones included in his poetry.

Nature has always been one of Torres favorite referents. This is particularly useful for him when writing his long series of love poems devoted to Mahalta, specially in the long series of "Cançó a Mahalta" (14, 17, 18, 20, 21, 64, 121, 139, 140). In all those poems he operates in a similar way: he uses as a correlative elements from nature to express the lovers situation at every stage. They are like "two parallel rivers" or their look ("esguard") is like a deep lake with quiet waters.

In one of the first "Cançó a Mahalta," Torres depicts two lovers in a "bosc de rondalla" (fairy tale forest), and nearby there is a city painted in gray and pink. It's an imaginary city presented as a dream setting where lovers meet.

The garden is already present from way before that. In poem 9, from October 1936, entitled "La torre," the garden is one of the elements stressed and that are useful to condense remembering, the distance between childhood and the present when he is writing. In "Ultima rosa," a November rose, born out of the right season becomes a symbol for uncertainty and the absurdity of fate. In "M'he despertat tot sol..." (29:65),[15] the garden is a prison, and it is also compared to paradise.

In the poem "Silenci en un jardí" (45:83) we are much closer to the heart of the matter. This sonnet and the following one, "Joia d'amor," may be read as a single unity because both discuss the problem of soul from a conditional perspective. Moreover: they introduce still a subject close to garden and city, that is labyrinth.[16]

> Si el silenci tingués una ànima, que endins
> viuria del seu cos! En la nit dels jardins,
>
> encarnada en el cercle més íntim d'una rosa,
> sentiria els estels tan enllà! Mig desclosa,
>
> tot li fóra frisança. Les ombres en els murs
> de les ciutats dorments, on els vivents obscurs
>
> respiren la nit... Lluny, el creixent de basarda
> d'un horitzó de porpra on el nou dia aguarda
>
> el seu exèrcit de remors... El desengany
> de cada fulla d'ombra que somnia el seu tany
>
> entre l'arbre i la llum... I desfer-se, ferida
> d'una aigua que s'escola, o d'un ocell que crida,
> amb un últim sentit per estimar l'esforç
> d'una aroma de rosa que arriba fins als morts...
> ("Silenci en un jardí")

I find extremely suggestive, and a truly innovative one, this association between Garden and City. It is also necessary to relate this so-called "garden poems" to the other voice in his poetry, the one attracted to social problems. Far from family and friends, Torres

witnessed some brutal events in his country, laying in bed without any
opportunity to do anything about it, facing death at any moment. His
poetry has many debts with his condition and personal situation. This
way can be read poems such as "Molt lluny d'aquí," "En la nit de Sant
Silvestre" or "La ciutat llunyana":[17]

> Ara que el braç, potent de les fúries aterra
> la ciutat d'ideals que volíem bastir,
> entre runes de somnis colgats, més prop de terra,
> Pàtria, guarda'ns:—la terra no sabrà mai mentir.

Here are sketched some of the coincidences between Torres and
some of the poets of his time: attitude towards language, the adaptation
of the garden and city topic, their interest in Symbolism. Màrius Torres
made once a rather radical confession to Carles Riba: "Si volgués
resumir què m'han portat aquests quatre anys darrers, us diria que, d'una
banda, l'afermament en la meva vocació, la consciència que jo sóc
essencialment aquesta cosa absurda: un poeta líric" (8).[18] And according
to what we have been able to read here Màrius Torres was not foreign
to Catalan poetical tradition ["t'apartes de la de tots els que a Catalunya
i en aquest segle t'han precedit en l'ús de la paraula," wrote Sales]. He
was not at all foreign but, on the other hand, very central to the
introduction of a Symbolism based upon structural association (the
famous Baudelaire's "correspondances") as Baudelaire himself, Mallar-
mé, or T.S. Eliot did. He was one of the first (and of the best) to write
this kind of hermetical poetry, cryptic, which demands an active role of
the reader. He made true the baudelarian idea of a "vident" poet, capable
of seeing through the material world into a world of ideal forms and
essences.

In one of his poems most devoted to absolute he wrote some
words that may work as a nice conclusion here:

> May joy invade my years again,
> without healing the wounds of my soul.
> O, Father of the Night, of the Ocean, and of Silence,
> it is peace I long for—not oblition.

Indeed his has been a work not forgotten.

Department of Spanish
Wellesley College
Wellesley, MA 02181

ENDNOTES

[1] Engl.: I know a city, very far from here, sweet and secret,/ where the years of joy are as brief as a night;/ where the sun is happy, where the wind is a poet,/ and where the fog is a faithful as my soul. (I quote from Francesc M. Franch, *A Catalan Symbolist. Selected Poems of Màrius Torres* [Peter Lang: New York, 1992])

[2] The first edition was published in Mexico in 1947 by Joan Sales (There is a 1992 facsimile by Paeria de Lleida). The second in 1950, in "Llibres de l'Ossa Menor" with a prologue by Carles Cardó; the third one had several new poems and a "Notícia biogràfica" by Joan Sales; the fourth one had still more new poems. The fifth edition, was published in 1977 by "Clàssics Catalans Ariel," added all the poems published by Mercè Boixareu in her book *Vida i obra de Màrius Torres*, Selecta, Barcelona, 1968. This edition had a prologue by Pere Gimferrer, and a "Cronologia" and a "Bibliografia" by Alfred Sargatal. The sixth edition has been published by Edicions 62 in 1993, with still new materials.

[3] Engl.: With your new style, after *Sweet Angel of Death*, you set yourself apart from all those who have preceded you, in Catalunya and in this age, in the use of the word, among whom there are so many illustrious and so many blessed ones; you set yourself apart not only by means of style and language, but above all by means of spirit. Your poetry is so lyric and so exclusively so that when you try out other types, narrative or descriptive, you fail. Lyric means subjective, personal, introverted, or it means nothing. Your best moments are precisely those which come closest to a midnight confession. In Catalunya and in our time there has been only one other style that was so, that of Salvat-Papasseit, so ignored by our most wise critics, but

only in random flashes... It is the case that the poetry of all of them
[the good Catalan poets of the twentieth century], with the only
exception of the best moments of Salvat-Papasseit, is mostly descriptive, narrative, decorative, patriotic or humorous and is more like a
literary exercise than a midnight confession.

⁴ Engl.: There is a certain "very Màrius" genre in which the stanzas,
alternating *alexandrines* and lines of other meters, are of a winged and
melodious music which expresses admirably the most difficult states
of spirit to explain.

⁵ Engl.: Do not awaken his sleep, do not move nor profane those
sleeping ashes, do not restore those fallen rocks because Beauty roots
there and nurtures with the recollections which assault it, and the
ruins are old and complete books, with their final page written.

⁶ Engl.: The scene represents an unkept garden, a classic garden, with
noble plants, ailing from neglect and conserving the mark of distinction which improvised gardens lack, a garden with the patina of age,
modeled by the kiss of time and impregnated with the sadness that
antique trees and deeply rooted plants impart. To one side, a circle of
cypress trees symmetrically trimmed, at the back a marble stairway
painted by the moss and with yellowish stone blocks; to the right, the
palace, with graffito figures half faded by rain; weeping willows and
cypress in the distance; closer to us, a drain for quiet and dead waters.

⁷ Engl.: Lying well on the ground, I like so much / to see before me in
a soft hillside / a verdant meadow beneath a blue sky! / And at the
poplars the great rustling / of the steel leaves which the wind raises /
with too many reflections of dazzling light // And the sun everywhere
/ and the brook falling / down the soft hillside /of the verdant
meadow beneath a blue sky. / All my limbs fallen, all of me on the
ground / emptied of all my force and empty of desire / thought leaves
me little by little. / And I start feeling so good there in the midst of
things / and an immense peace invades me / and I feel one more piece
of the soft meadow / verdant, verdant beneath a blue sky.

⁸ Engl.: Now I see above the mountain range of fire our pine / oh
people who make your path through the golden fields! / It takes me by
surprise like a wine / the old humble power which unites us. / (It is
alive as the broom and like sky blue / your fuss, oh Catalan girl) //
You smile at sunset, white farm houses/ between haystacks that keep
good company / and every farmhouse is surrounded / by a small
forest, hay, vineyards and an edge with three polls. // I would like,
while getting lost through valleys /say your beauty, oh land of health!
/ among darks things and forgotten lives/ like this cricket that sings

in a lost path.

[9] Engl.: La Côte d'Azur is not a myth. St. Raphael, the first town, is delicious. Soft mountain peaks, the color of copper at the edges, and blue at heart, make an ample and deep cove, like a great river halted. The houses are ample and red with orange groves and geraniums. Strategically located, a bit a green, of pine.

[10] Engl.: You who love the humble garden of Puig d'Olena / where the burnt trees stand in abundance / between the sky and the rock and the house and the woods. / The mountain garden, noble and rough, / Mercè, I want to tell you of the springtime / timid, smiling, and light / which inserts in the severe landscape of this country / the positive and tender grace of a smile.

[11] Engl.: The dusk silences the innumerable shouts, / metallic, gray, of the city and lets / one feel the loving complaint in the shadow / of those arriving late. // Melancholy interior: lost / are the limits now, vaguely endures / a tearful sound between the quietude / dawn of the moon in the rose bushes glow.

[12] Engl.: I, now, live in the square garden / of a day old enough so it no longer invokes / ghosts of the past nor the sunset.

[13] Engl.: Ah, roads separate us / and pastures without green grass / landscape of mannequin / and little mountains of ashes.

[14] Engl.: Memory distances those fine afternoons / guided, youthful steps / along the long paths polls, palm trees, air / lake, birds, sunset, wind, dialogue, / fountain, poplar, bank, and the candid circle / of fragile girls trembling aware / full of play, suddenly running away.

[15] Engl.: I have opened my eyes, alone in an ancient garden, / not knowing if it is a prison or my realm.

[16] Engl.: If silence had a soul, how far within / its body would I live. On the night of the gardens / embodied in the most intimate circle of a rose / I would feel the stars so distant! Half opened / all was longing to the rose. The shadows on the walls / of the sleeping cities where the dark inhabitants / breathe the night. Far, the growing terror / of a horizon of purple where the new day waits for / its army of murmurs. Disillusion / of every leaf of shadow which dreams its sucker / between the tree and the light ... And to become undone, wounded / by water which runs, or by a bird which cries / with one last meaning for loving the power of a rose's aroma which reaches the dead.

[17] Engl.: Now that the powerful arm of the furies scares / the ideal which we wanted to build / amidst ruins of hung dreams, closer to the earth / homeland, await us—the earth will never know how to lie.

[18] Engl.: If I wanted to summarize what it is that these last four years have brought to me, I would say, on one hand, conviction in my vocation, consciousness that I am essentially this absurd thing: a lyric poet.

Works cited

Gimferrer, Pere. "Introducció" a Màrius Torres, *Poesies*. Barcelona: Ariel, 1978.

Harbison, Robert. *Eccentric Spaces*. New York, A. A. Knopf, 1977.

Pàmies, Jordi. *Temes principals en la poesia de Màrius Torres*. "Reduccions" 16 (maig 1982): 71-90.

Prats, Margarida. "Introducció" a Màrius Torres, in *Poesies i altres escrits*. Barcelona: Edicions 62, 1993.

Pugh, Simon. *Garden-Nature-Language*, Manchester: Manchester U. P., 1988.

Sales, Joan. *Cartes a Màrius Torres*. Barcelona: Club editor, 1976.

Torres, Màrius. "Cartes a Joan Sales," in Màrius Torres, *Poesies*. Barcelona: Ariel, 1978: 213-248.

Torres, Màrius. "Correspondència a Carles Riba," in Màrius Torres, *Poesies*. Barcelona: Ariel, 1978: 249-263.

Peter Cocozzella

AGUSTÍ BARTRA'S TRANSCENDENTAL EXILE

Agustí Bartra (1908-1982) is the author of a sizeable collection of poems and prose works, written for the most part in his native Catalan. He came of age in the mid 1930s and was deeply affected by the ravages of the Spanish Civil War (1936-1939). Together with a number of coetaneous Catalan authors—Pere Calders, Salvador Espriu, Mercè Rodoreda, Joan Sales, Joan Teixidor, Joan Vinyoli, to name but a representative few—Bartra belongs to that group of Spanish writers known as members of the Generation of 1936.[1] As a soldier in the Republican Army, he experienced combat firsthand and was driven to exile, the dire consequence of defeat. His personal odyssey took him through France, the Dominican Republic, Cuba, until he finally settled in Mexico. From Mexico he traveled to the United States where, on three different occasions, he resided as a Guggenheim scholar.[2] In spite or, perhaps, because of these unsettling events of his youth and early adulthood, Bartra managed to rise above the history of man's inhumanity to man. Early in his career he became inspired by his illustrious predecessor, Joan Maragall (1860-1911). In emulation of Maragall's distinctive "voice" and "living word"—the *veu* par excellence and the *paraula* viva—Bartra fashioned a poetic all his own. He sensed the incarnation of that *veu* in a multifarious persona, evoked age-old myths, and created brand new ones. His prolific Muse took refuge in a visionary

world, capturing, in the sweep of cosmopolitanism, echoes from Pablo
Neruda's prophetic vein, Jorge Guillén's or Vicente Aleixandre's
fascination with the plenitude of being, Walt Whitman's egocentricism,
Ezra Pound's, Hart Crane's, William Carlos Williams's all-encompassing
textuality.[3] Agustí Bartra fulfills, perhaps better than any other Spanish
writer of 36, Northrop Frye's definition of the "encyclopaedic form."[4]
Even a cursory review of his masterpieces—*Màrsias i Adila* (1948: a
paean to the quintessential soldier), *Quetzalcòatl* (1971: a recasting of the
Nahuatl myth), and the trilogy of *Soleia* (1976: a conjoining of Herman
Melville's Captain Ahab with some personages conjured from Catalan
folklore)—reveals the wide range of Bartra's poetic vision.

In the poem "El fill pròdig" ('The Prodigal Son'), one of the
components of *Els himnes* ('*Hymns,*' 1974), Bartra presents a free
adaptation of the parable from Luke's Gospel. A returnee to the
fatherland, the poem's persona reflects Bartra himself who, afflicted with
mostalgia, put an end to his own thirty-one-year exile on January 11,
1970. The persona in question projects himself, with great relish, into the
role of a mentor of future generations. Turning aside from the miseries
of the human condition, he prefers to capitalize upon the buoyancy of
hope that springs eternal. The Prodigal Son mututates into a veritable
Messiah. The dedication to León Felipe invites a comparison with that
other notable Spanish *transterrado* of the Franco regime. In contrast with
Felipe, who died away from his beloved country, the bard envisaged by
Bartra would not vanish like the proverbial "vox clamantis in deserto."

Bartra himself advances a memorable definition for his distinctive
poetic voice. In a letter to the young Catalan poet, Miquel Desclot,
Bartra draws a sharp distinction between the mere *paraula* and the
personal *veu*. He presupposes an exclusive bond between authentic poetry
and the sense of time embedded in the *veu*: "la poesia no és pas la
paraula, encara que sense paraules no és possible de fer poesia, sinó el

temps existencial i vivencial" (*Sobre poesia* 202). He is quite precise in determining the origin of *la veu* charged with poetry at the exact moment in which the heart and the spirit spring into action: "La *veu* potser comença en el poeta quan s'ha acabat la tasca de l'ull i es fa necessària la del cor, l'esperit i la consciència vivencial" (*Sobre poesia* 203). In a fitting conclusion Bartra envisages his notion of a spiritualized *veu* as the revelation, *sub specie aeternitatis,* of a process of sublimation which begins with down-to-earth existence and culminates into a transcendental state of grace: "però l'autèntic 'honneur de l'homme' no és, crec jo, 'la sainte parole' valeryana, sinó la *veu* que funda i esdevé epifania des d'aquella coincidència entre les noces del sentit de la terra i l'esperit de l'home en funció de visió i eternitat..." (*Sobre poesia* 204).

By advancing a theory of a special strain of twentieth-century Catalan literature, stretching between Maragall and Bartra with Joan Salvat-Papasseit as intermediary, Desclot underscores the deepseated empathy which Bartra feels toward Maragall's living presence: "Sentim Maragall prop de nosaltres, convivent, actual..." (*Sobre poesia* 23, Desclot 11-2). From Maragall Bartra derives two fundamental traits: a kinetics of transcendence and a steadfast striving toward the quintessence of all things (language in particular). Bartra's poetry mirrors, then, Maragall's paradoxical reconciliation between universalism (the poet's general appeal to his fellow human beings) and dialectalism (the subjective lyricism inspired by the soul of the people—*el alma del pueblo,* to use one of Maragall's favorite phrases) (Vilanova 52-63). On the basis of these two Maragallian qualities, Bartra, as he clearly states in *Sobre poesia,* conceived his plan of the "Gran Cant de l'Home" (32). The "Cant" in question draws its vitality, the author tells us, from "l'esperit de la poesia," which "s'afua cap a la transcendència de la vida total" (38). At the same time, he cherished his notion of "la humanitat essencial" (31) and "les més profundes realitats" (32). Throughout his career Bartra honed his skills in tackling the symbiosis between the individual and society. He endeavored to come to grips with the conflict between harsh reality and hard-to-reach ideals and with the tensions arising from the brutal impact of personal and communal crises. Borrowing Rodríguez Monegal's astute comments apropos of Pablo Neruda's aesthetics, we may observe that, not unlike Neruda and some other authors (Goethe among them) that Monegal also brings into the equation, Bartra "combina sin descaracterizarse, asume nuevas máscaras para expresar mejor la persona única, huye para quedarse siempre clavado en su mismo centro" (64).

In 1938 Bartra published his first collection of poems, entitled *Cant corporal*.[5] Through this showpiece of low-key rhetoric, ("la retórica de tono menor," as Pío Baroja would have it), he filtered out life's raw passions without losing a direct feel of the ambiance of the Civil War. He anticipated what Carlos Bousoño calls "la poesía afectivo-conceptual" (92)—the poetry, that is, of a realistic mode, which Bousoño himself defines in terms of the admixture of affective and conceptual rather than sensorial elements. Bartra's *Cant corporal*—the title itself, as Francesc Vallverdú suspects, comes as an ironic response to Maragall's *Cant espiritual* (Vallverdú 46)—harbingers Dámaso Alonso's *Hijos de la ira* (1944) and Aleixandre's *Historia del corazón* (1954). At the same time it is reminiscent of the historic manifesto, "Sobre una poesía sin pureza," which Neruda published in Madrid in 1935 in order to propound a poetry of flesh and blood, "gastada," in Neruda's own words, "como por un ácido por los deberes de la mano, penetrada por el sudor y el humo, oliente a orina y azucena, salpicada por las diversas profesiones que se ejercen dentro y fuera de la ley" (quoted in Rodríguez Monegal 76-77).

In the light of these auspicious beginnings, one may have expected Bartra to become a leading exponent, among the Spanish writers of 36, of that same type of "poesía sin pureza" vigorously championed by

Neruda. The critic Saul Yurkievich relates this kind of poetry to one of the two generating principles of the Chilean poet's *Canto general* and defines it with the label of "realismo historicista." This is, in Yurkievich's words, "la poesía militante-testimonial, regida por una voluntad política y pedagógica" (199). Bartra, nevertheless, opted for another route. Apparently, he found "realismo historicista" inimical to the Maragallian *veu*, toward which he felt a natural affinity and irresistible attraction. Much more in tune with the *veu* that resounded in the depths of Bartra's soul were such works as Guillén's *Cántico* (second edition, 1936), Aleixandre's *La destrucción o el amor* (1935), and *Residencia en la tierra* (1925-1935) by none other than Neruda. Particularly inspiring for Bartra must have been the notion of "la vida como fuente, la plenitud del ser y la plenitud de la palabra," which José Manuel Blecua identifies with these very words in Guillén's *Cántico* (Blecua 12). Doubtless, Bartra was familiar, also, with Aleixandre's tellurian and cosmic imagery and with Neruda's discourse of the mythic prophet. Deeply stirred by these inspiring authors (Guillén, Aleixandre, Neruda himself), Bartra experienced a drastic change of heart toward his *Cant corporal* and toward the aesthetic for which it stood. Both book and aesthetic he came to repudiate once and for all. Thus, the Bartra deeply involved, as a soldier and exile, in the Civil War and its aftermath, the Bartra profoundly sensitive to the poignant realities alluded to in Neruda's manifesto of 1935, the Bartra endowed with an ideal background and aptitude to become a *comprometido, historicista, engagé* poet, decided, in spite of it all, to make a clear break with *compromiso, historicismo,* and *engagement.*

In *L'arbre de foc* (1946) and *L'evangeli del vent* (1956), Bartra's *veu* accrues in depth and intensity: it becomes the compendium of an actual existence rooted in temporal circumstances although ultimately projected unto a sphere of timelessness. "Als llavis del silenci" ('Upon

the Lips of Silence'), the opening poem of *L'evangeli al vent*, provides
an apt introduction to Bartra's post-Romantic, Nerudian verve. In Part
II of "Als llavis" we read:

> I l'espai, a l'entorn, de solitud s'inunda.
> Morir del cant ardent—l'inevitable vol
> que arbora el suprem èxtasi de l'alosa jocunda—,
>
> tot corbant-me de nou a la pàl·lida estrella
> que ja anuncia als mots l'arribada del sol.
> Oh dia meu: atònit esguard sense parpella (1: 106).[6]

Bartra's persona would provide ample illustration for Monegal's
enlightening remarks concerning "Arte poética," the all-important poem
in Neruda's *Residencia en la tierra* of 1933:

> Los seis versos finales del poema sintetizan una estética de la
> poesía como profecía, de la poesía como algo que está surgiendo
> del fondo más abismal del mundo y del poeta, de la poesía como
> iluminación, como rito y como salvación (69).

The prophet, the universal "I" of the poet, and the Wordsworthian
primordial child epitomize signal aspects of yet another stage in the
evolution of Bartra's aesthetics: the mythification of he poet's persona.
The myth that constantly looms in the horizon of Bartra's wide vision is
that of a poet as a superman or a demigod. For a fitting portrait of this
personage in all his cosmic grandeur we need look no further than
Aleixandre's own prologue to his *La destrucción o el amor* (second
edition). That great Spanish master of the "encyclopaedic form" makes
the following observation:

> El poeta está lleno de sabiduría, pero no puede envanecerse porque
> quizá no es suya: una fuerza incognoscible, un espíritu habla por
> su boca. Con los dos pies hincados en la tierra, una corriente
> prodigiosa se condensa, se agolpa bajo sus plantas para correr por

su cuerpo y alzarse por su lengua. Es entonces la tierra misma. la tierra profunda, la que llama por ese cuerpo arrebatado. Pero otras veces el poeta ha crecido, ahora hacia lo alto, y con su frente incrustada en un cielo habla con voz estelar, con cósmica resonancia, mientras está sintiendo en su pecho el soplo mismo de los astros (Quoted in Bousoño 55).

Bartra's production both before and after his return to Catalonia attests to numerous examples of his multifarious treatment of the mythic mode. Already in *L'arbre de foc* and *L'evangeli del vent* he imaginatively elaborates various ingredients: the Biblical story of Ruth ("Poema de Rut"), some details from the *Odyssey* ("Poemes d'Odisseu"), and the intuition of the primeval marriage between man and woman ("Poemes d'Anna"). After these early attempts, he gave free rein to his fertile imagination in creating or re-creating myths which inform works of major proportions, such as the aforementioned *Quetzalcòatl* and *Màrsias i Adila*, included in vol. I of his *Obra poètica completa*. The same may be said of the masterpieces—*Soleia, L'home auroral, El gos geomètric*—contained in vol. II of that same publication. We realize that disparate ingredients become grist for the mill of Bartra's versatile inventiveness: besides the items derived from the Bible, the Homeric epics, and the legends of the Nahuatl god-poet, there are the formidable figures conjured up from home-grown legends (Garí and *comte* Arnau) and from the mystery-laden ambiance of Herman Melville's narratives (Captain Ahab). In *El gos geomètric* Bartra even tries his hand at refurbishing Shakespeare's deptiction of Caliban, thus gaining insight into the dark side of the human spirit. He is equally adept in bringing to life creations of his own vintage, investing each of them with the depth and exemplarity of a prototype: witness the Maiden of Undying Hope (Soleia), the soldier Màrsias and his beloved Adila, the Man of Dawn ("L'home Auroral") and his female counterpart (Vidala).[7]

While not losing sight of the Messiah, the prophet, and the heroic demigod, Bartra employs his talents in a pluralistic approach to myth-making. Among the Spanish authors of the twentieth century, Valle-Inclán is one of the few who can vie with him in proliferating epiphanies of the superego. Only a superficial reading, then, can account for the pitfall incurred by those critics who, despite Bartra's own protestation to the contrary, regard Walt Whitman as his main if not exclusive inspiration. Upon close scrutiny Bartra's creativity proves to be as complex as his sources are numerous and wide-ranging. Since the early 1940s Bartra had been an avid reader and translator of American poetry and had spent the period between 1949 and 1950 preparing his bilingual (English-Catalan) anthology of that poetry, which he published in 1951. This indicates that, in addition to Whitman, he studied a host of other American authors whose influence he did not shun.

One can hardly overemphasize the bond of empathy that Bartra must have felt toward those salient American poets, whose characteristics he himself identified as follows: "consciència social, voluntat més o menys concreta de crear el mite d'Amèrica i necessitat d'expressar-se usant termes de validesa humana" (Bartra, *Una antologia* 6). A meticulous study of Bartra's sources would reveal specific traces not only of Whitman but also of the leading exponents of American literature between the wars (1914-45)—Ezra Pound, Edwin Arlington Robinson, Robert Frost, Carl Sandburg, Wallace Stevens, T. S. Eliot, Hart Crane, William Carlos Williams, among others. Bartra is much indebted to these writers for some key symbols and devices attendant upon his mythopoetic enterprise. Strictly from the literary tradition of the United States Bartra derives his attitude toward Nature and Mother Earth—"la idea gairebé metafísica de la terra," as Murià calls it, and his notion of woman as, again in Murià's words, "femenina, maternal i tel·lúrica" (*L'obra de Bartra* 35).

Bartra has created—who can doubt it?—a wondrous literary universe. His insistence on a rarefied aesthetic of the visionary raises some questions as to whether that universe would readily find an ontological correlative in the day-to-day flow of the history of our time. Does Bartra, in effect, choose to circumvent history altogether? How does his poetic world relate to his own experience as an exile? Like many other fellow expatriates he did not lack the awareness that the circumstances of the exile often give birth to a compelling desire to escape from the unsavory realities of the kingdom of this world. What is unique about Bartra is that he learns to transform that awareness into a challenge for a momentum of expansion toward a textuality of multiculturalism. At the heart of his multicultural text lies the Homeric prototype. Bartra's quasi mystical transport reminds us of John Keats's enthusiasm "on first looking into Chapman's Homer," to quote the epigraph of Keats's splendid sonnet. "Much have I traveled in the realms of gold," exclaims the English poet's entranced persona, "and many goodly states and kingdoms seen." Bartra feels no less strongly than does Keats the allure of those voyages "in the realms of gold."

But how, we may still ask, does Bartra relate the immanence of his pilgrimage to the transcendence of the prototype eminently exemplified by the Homeric epic? Without indulging ourselves in facile analogies, we will bear in mind that what Bartra transcends is precisely the sense of the quotidian stresses of a transplanted *vivencia*. In 1953, at the most intense point of his inspiration from Classical Greek antiquity, he produced not an *Odyssey*, but, rather, an *Odisseu*. This *Odisseu* is a typical text of Bartra's in that it lacks the adventuresome verve of an episodic structure. Indeed, it lacks a plot altogether. It is a striking, idiosyncratic combination of epic proportion and lyrical élan. Bartra manages to recapture the Odyssean spirit in a non-narrative superstructure that allows the poetic voice to sing epically and lyrically all at once and become incarnated in the persona of Bartra's hero par excellence. It is in that persona where we perceive the grand struggle between the transcendental and the immanent.

In the final analysis, Bartra is attuned to the same tragic conflict that Salvador Espriu, the other outstanding poet of 36, dramatizes in the portrayal of his own alter ego, Salom de Sinera. Here an important distinction needs to be made: while Bartra pursues the larger-than-life image of the myth, Espriu, a champion, after all, of the inner exile, strives for the definition of a psychic space—the interior theater of what Unamuno would call "el sentimiento trágico de la vida." Adapting to his purpose techniques he borrows from Unamuno and, even more significantly, from Calderón de la Barca, Espriu, in his memorable book entitled *El caminant i el mur* (1954), depicts his tragic persona, who, in the midst of his desolation is haunted by visions of splendid mansions:

> I em perdo i sóc, sense missatge, sol,
> enllà del cant, enmig dels oblidats
> caiguts amb por, només un somni fosc
> que va sortir dels palaus de la llum (1: 354).

Espriu's protagonist echoes the lament of Segismundo, who, in the confinement of his own prison reminisces about his dwelling—an ephemeral one, to be sure—amid the splendors of the royal palace. Espriu's counterpart for Calderón's hero asserts his presence through a paradoxical silent cry, which resounds with a deafening blare through the caverns of the self and, with that cry, attests to his headlong descent into the abyss within his mind. The abyss, we soon learn, is a private Hell conditioned by an existential flaw, designated by the metaphysical term "mancament."

Despite the parallelism we may discern between Espriu and Bartra, the differences between the two poets is considerable. The enlightening comments derived from Michael Ugarte's recent study on the literature of the Spanish *desterrados,* victims of the Civil War, help us appreciate that difference. Ugarte brings to light the special significance of the motif of the fall in that literature. Taking his cue from the Augustinian juxtaposition of exile and the notion of a collapse into a God-forsaken "abyss of unlikeness," Ugarte sees the same motif repeated across the ages by exiles as diverse as Dante and the Jewish poet Edmond Jabès (27-30). Espriu, we now realize, surrenders to the haunting leitmotif so perceptively analyzed by Ugarte: Espriu, we hasten to add, but not Bartra. The latter well may turn out to be unique among his cohorts in that his expression conveys the overall thrust not of a fall but of an uplift. The fundamental difference between Espriu and Bartra parallels, to some extent, the divergent orientation exhibited by each writer's respective wellspring of inspiration: Unamuno for Espriu and Maragall for Bartra.

The Maragallian thrust that characterizes most of Bartra's production, if not all of it, acquires a special urgency, as one would expect, after his return to the motherland. Murià points out that *Poemes del retorn* and *Els himnes*, published, respectively, in 1972 and 1974, "tenen la qualitat d'himnes perquè responen a la necessitat d'expansió del poeta ple de goig i eufòria i salut física en la plenitud de la possessió de tot això que ara el volta i que havia enyorat" (*L'obra de Bartra* 273). Bartra, then, comes home to an experience of plenitude, to a consciousness, complete and satisfying, of an integrated self, reconciled with past history and present circumstance, in sublime harmony with society and with the whole world. Focussing particularly on the poetry that Bartra produced immediately after his return, Murià expounds, as follows, on the observations we have just quoted:

> S'hi troba encara aquell embadaliment admirat, joiós i sorprès davant el mar i els camps retrobats: «mar de recomençament», «el meu dia salvat»... El sentir-se jove quan surt a veure el mar...
> (*L'obra de Bartra* 273)

Bartra basks in a sense of rejuvenation and fulfilled destiny.

In the translated passages included in the appendix below I should like to offer to the English-speaking reader a token of Bartra's latest production. The passages, I believe, encapsulate the salient modes and moods of Bartra's poetry. In the excerpts from *L'evangeli al vent* and from the "Rapsòdia d'Ahab" the bard modulates, now ever so softly, now full blast, the organ music that spans the wide gamut of the epic and the elegy. The epic overtones linger in the remaining selection, "Rapsò-dia de Garí," but the elegiac harmony shifts into the thunderous dissonance of a Shakespearean tragedy à la *King Lear*. Here Bartra profiles, with striking immediacy, the gigantic frame a Catalan Mephis-topheles, who dares cry out, *de profundis,* in stentorian strains. What with its attendant theatricality and outward projection, Garí's voice resounds as a natural complement to that stifled cry ("el crit amagat") that Espriu challenges us to take up from his Salom agonistes, withdrawn into a labyrinth of loneliness. Through Garí and Salom we will learn to appreciate the immanence of the Catalan exilic experience as incarnated in two memorable figures. All differences aside, their powerful expressions hold in store the élan of a journey into transcendency.

Dept. of Romance Languages
Binghamton University
Binghamton, N.Y. 13902

ENDNOTES

[1] A competent discussion of this generation within the historiography of modern Catalan letters may be found in Fuster 339-51.

[2] In her two seminal books—*Crònica de la vida d'Agustí Bartra* and *L'obra de Bartra: assaig d'aproximació* (cf. the bibliography be-low)—Bartra's wife, Anna Murià, provides a complete review of his

career and literary production.

[3] In "La veu, la persona i el mite: cap a la definició d'una estètica d'Agustí Bartra," I analyze the birth and evolution of the salient traits of Bartra's poetry.

[4] For a full discussion of the "encyclopaedic" as opposed to the "episodic" form, see Frye 52-67, 315-26.

[5] Eventually, this booklet was repudiated by the its author: see Murià, *L'obra de Bartra* 185-6.

[6] For a translation of these verses, see the appendix below.

[7] An updated commentary on Bartra's latest post-exilic production may be found in Desclot, Introducció.

APPENDIX

(Passages from Agustí Bartra's Poetry, trans. Peter Cocozzella)

[N.B.: The numerals at the end of each excerpt refer to the volume and pagination in Bartra's *Obra poètica completa* (cf. the bibliographic note below)].

I. *L'evangeli al vent* (1956)

Excerpt from "Als llavis del silenci"

I

Oh nights! Such hibernation in immobile messages
—made out of the heart and adieus!—waiting for the words
that to each image bring existence on the wing.
And sightless masks beneath the wind of sighs!

Increate world of the song: profound valley offered
to luminous forests of giant summer seasons.
O constellation pure, music which is awakened
like a tree on the bank of a great dream of rivers.

To float in sweet abandon forever on the drift,
wafted by royal waters, a slave of the last ice
of silence that enfolds the fugitive, a prow.

Oh, what a thought still harvests darkness without defense
and the soul keeps threshing celestial spikes of wheat!
O zenith of the poem, o jewel free, immense!

II

O voices! The mouth too harsh invades the ethereal
refuge of my heart. O fount of stellar sap
flowing into the nocturnal hearing of mystery!
The silence leans onto its mortal imprint.

Let's sing the tree of the cry! To stretch the branch and the
                                                      [fruit
to the eternal menace of the gelid night
of a being that abandons all lucid struggle.
Birds of our conscience! Let's sing the tree of the cry!

And, all around, the space is drowned in solitude.
Let's die of the burning song—the inevitable flight
that lifts the joyful lark in ecstasy sublime—,

as I bend, once again, toward the gleam of pallid starlight
which to the words announces the arrival of the sun.
Behold my day: astonished stare that has no eyelid!

                                                   (1: 105-6)

II. *Soleia: les tres rapsòdies* (1977)

A. Excerpt from "Rapsòdia d'Ahab"

Here comes the mist, the mist procreated on the peaks.
Stabbed by lightening bolts, the mist now sleeps, now walks,
and moves down to search the heart of the poppy
and of the yellow history of countless crops of wheat.

She grazes the great oak, an escort in his fortress,
and buries the bird's flight in her mobile cottony garments.
She wears a poor man's tatters and a thousand watery masks,
the rosemary perfumes her feet, the feet of a dainty damsel,
her dress rips now and again on the branch which lies asleep.
A man will never stop and drink from her jet-black cup,
a man who is ensnared by the spell of the impalpable witch:
he holds his steps and feels his way, walking through the mist,
which neither speaks of death nor of funereal wings.
The man who curbs his steps, who tightens up his hopes,
makes sure he carries still the bread inside his satchel,
his knife now tucked away to sleep within its sheath.
Perhaps he'll close his eyes and with a slow anxiety
will raise his hand and bury it within his flowing locks
staple grain for his dream world:
he will inspect the valley, a heart in its contour,
touching with his five fingers a nationhood of words;
and he will hear resounding arboreal elegies,
while lying by a narrow brook running with living water:
he expects the wind to eradicate that grassy smile of his....
Ill omens are all around. Reclining upon the meadow,
the man perhaps listens to a fleeting voice
or hears the slow thrust, up high, of the eagle's flight
and contemplates the fall of the mist
beheaded by the sun's sword....

Ahab and Soleia
come out of the mist.
The sun is like
a crown of honeybees.

And the firs lean forward.
What an air of clover
and camomile
we breathe along the ridges!

Ahab and Soleia
have forgotten the mist.
The larks are far away
and the song of the blackbird.

And the snows draw near,
and the clouds desert their posts,
and the air takes off its rings
and sheds light upon the peaks.

THE VOICES OF THE EARTH

Ahab, though tall, you are now stooping
and the winds now make you bend;
your crystalline beard is good-looking,
from your eyes beams of light you send.

Now your ocean is nowhere in sight:
it's a vast memory, lost in the distance.
By your sheer stature and in a new light
firm as a rock will be your stance.

Upward you strive day in and day out,
and there you stand, right next to the ice.
The ant and the giant are having their bout,
while you keep biting the skies.

I'm sure you're accostumed to waves of green,
I know what remorse the seed can bear.
But roots in your travels I've never seen
—travels, orphans of fear.

You thrived in the battle, hand to hand,
with sea and space,
as always you turned your back to the land,
the eternal brand of "never" on your face.

What hostile sky would bleed your side?
You have survived from your dire plight!
Your wish to inherit must now subside
—to inherit the star that weeps in white!

You show nostalgia, doubtless, titanic,
you, backward walker, worse than Cain;
but in your heart, a rose oceanic,
death will smite the hurricane.

We are the heralds of the tree,
the grass, the fount, the roof, the fold.
Lovers of cold marble we'll never be,
in furrows we grow old.

In the hustle and bustle we make our dwelling
and gently comb a wing of mud.
All matter is an idyll worth the telling,
a song of blood.

Our only law is life, we own,
a pinch of gold dust
on ice-cold ashes thrown,
and death will grin, we trust!

Near threshing grounds we keep love's wake,
an age-old yearning, a road of gloom;
a great ambush the apple groves make,
and they're about to bloom.
O ancient mariner, ye shriveled artichoke,
ye rod of wintry steel,
Ahab, Ahab, give up—don't joke!—
the sea-grey stanza, the loneliness you feel.

The blue in the far-off horizon,
give it up for youthful gold.
Mother Earth is the only friend one relies on,
nice thighs of prime fiber, a matrix for a heart that is bold.

Ahab of action and martyrdom, pay heed
to the sun's dice above the herbage,
to the rainbow's arrow, alive, indeed,
unfailing remedy—that's my message!

Now, far away from algae and flags,
the open summit will be your nest.
From the meadows you'll get bliss without snags
and from the river, rest.

(2: 312-5)

B. Excerpt from "Rapsòdia de Garí"

... hurray for me, hurray for me, Gari, hobbling along, a
puppet free to choose for himself and die, who sticks out his
tongue and thumbs his nose—hah, hah, hah—at violins and
obese monuments, me, me, Gari, bereft of echo, sparrow hawk
in the mist, a lark in horizontal flight—hey-hey-hey-hey!
-raucous amidst the tortures from my male hunger and female
thirst, yea, also was I looking for the red bird in the sky... The
bird...? What am I saying? Fire and blood were warbling
within my eye? Right inside my eye...? Oh, yea! That, also!
Hee-hee!... and that's why I have been living my life groping
between desire and shadow, and, now and then, I'd fall like
Paul-Lee-Famous, and did not know where I was falling, with
long clownish feet I would try out the ladder, the dim descent,
and would leave behind the greyish range of sleepless hours,
like sweatshops in ancient slums, and down, down I'd go, with
flabby legs and arms, a wreckage of all my instincts, and
would see vague lights like splotches of semen, lightening bolts
in a squatting posture, Perfloating lamps and anonymous
sufferings like rabbit pelts dried up and still embedded into an
old wall...I'd fall and, then, get up. I'd weep beneath the tree
of nails and sponges, and way up there, from the inaccessible
sky of my childhood, my laughter hung down just like a
flower...

And I would run away, run away from persistent assaults:
fangs, drivel, and vinegar, and from the vulture and the lance
aimed at my flank, and my big wide eye would rain with
tears—would drench my shadow, half hunchback, half bell, my
shadow so heavy of a puppet of lead, and down, down, down
I fell, disjointed and scattered—don't you hear me, dear
mother?

O wind, you are forever nuzzling,O dog in the dunghill, O
night, O spinster moon, —O sun, to shine more, you flagellate
yourself—and the sea, full of rancor... —O sea, ye iron-hearted
hag, in your boundless litter, let loose colic, whimper, and
rebuke... Do you hear me? (2: 123-4)

Works Cited

Bartra, Agustí. *Obra poètica completa.* I: 1938-1972. 2ª ed. Ed. Llorenç Soldevila. Barcelona: Edicions 62, 1984.

---. *Obra poètica completa.* II: 1972-1982. Ed. Miquel Desclot. Barcelona: Edicions 62, 1983.

---. *Sobre poesia.* Ed. Miquel Desclot. Barcelona: Laia, 1980.

---, ed. i trad. *Una antologia de la lírica nord-americana.* Mèxic: Ed. Lletres, 1951.

Blecua, José Manuel. Introducción. *Cántico* [1936]. Barcelona: Labor, 1970.

Bousoño, Carlos. *La poesía de Vicente Aleixandre.* 2ª ed. Madrid: Gredos, 1956.

Cocozzella, Peter. "La veu, la persona i el mite: cap a la definició d'una estètica d'Agustí Bartra." Rasico and Wittlin 245-65.

Desclot, Miquel. Introducció. *Obra poètica completa.* II: 1972-1982. By Agustí Bartra. Ed. Miquel Desclot. Barcelona: Edicions 62, 1983. 11-61.

---. Pròleg. *Sobre poesia.* 5-13.

Espriu, Salvador. *Obres completes.* 5 vols. Ed. Francesc Vallverdú. Barcelona: Edicions 62, 1985-1990.

Frye, Northrop. *Anatomy of Criticism: Four Essays.* 1957. New York: Athcncum, 1969.

Fuster, Joan. *Literatura catalana contemporània.* Barcelona: Curial,

1972.

Montané, Mireia, ed. *Lliçons de literatura comparada catalana i castellana (segles XIX-XX)*. Barcelona, 1982. Montserrat: Abadia, 1985.

Murià, Anna. *Crònica de la vida d'Agustí Bartra*. 2ª ed. Andorra la Vella: Serra Airosa, 1983.

---. *L'obra de Bartra: assaig d'aproximació*. Barcelona: Vosgos, S.A., 1975.

Rasico, Philip D., and Curt J. Wittlin, eds. *Actes del Cinquè Col·loqui d'Estudis Catalans a Nord-Amèrica* (Tampa-St. Augustine, 1987). Montserrat: Abadia, 1989.

Rodríguez Monegal, Emir. "El sistema del poeta." Rodríguez Monegal and Santí 53-91.

Rodríguez Monegal, Emir, and Enrico Mario Santí, eds. *Pablo Neruda*. Madrid: Taurus, 1980.

Ugarte, Michael. *Shifting Ground: Spanish Civil War Exile Literature*. Durham: Duke U.P., 1989.

Vallverdú, Francesc. *Escrits sobre poetes i poesia*. Manacor: Ajuntament—Caixa de Balears, 1985.

Vilanova, Antonio. "Maragall y Juan Ramón Jiménez". Montané 49-86.

Yurkievich, Saul. "Mito e historia: dos generadores del 'Canto general'." Rodríguez Monegal i Santí 198-218.

Roberto J. González-Casanovas

RACIONERO GRAU'S NEOMEDIEVAL MYTH OF RAMON LLULL: POSTMODERN IDEOLOGY IN CATALAN HISTORICAL FICTION

I. New history/historicism and new medievalism.

This study examines the postmodern uses and interpretations of medieval cultural history that are represented in Racionero Grau's historical novel about Ramon Llull (1232-1316): *Raimon o el seny fantàstic* (1985). Postmodernism is generally understood to include a redefinition of the boundaries between text and context, an eclecticism in forms of expression, the critique of codes of authority, and the pursuit of cultural relativism in interpretation (cf. Brownlee et al., Burke, Veeser, and Zumthor). For Racionero Grau, the equally historical and mythical figure of Llull offers a text and context for the new Catalanism and Mediterranean crosscultural studies, as well as a pretext and subtext for advocacy of a new medievalism within postmodernism. Not only is Llull an extraordinary figure who has fascinated many propagandists, writers of legend, and romancers over the centuries, but he has also become an emblem in the twentieth century for various ideological positions in Catalonia, Spain, and abroad: as someone beatified by the Catholic Church who at one time was condemned by the Inquisition, he stands for both orthodoxy and heterodoxy; as a lay reformer of the Christian missions to the Muslims of the Mediterranean, he embodies both the expansion of

Christendom and the dialogue with Islam; and as a systematic and mystical advocate of the union of faith, reason, and love, who betrays the eccentricities of an autodidact and propagandist, he has come to represent both the marginality of a Catalan gnosis in the thirteenth century dominated by Thomas Aquinas and the typicality of a Catalan synthesis within the age of Mediterranean-Iberian *convivència* promoted by Frederick II of Sicily, Alfonso X of Castile, and James I of Aragon. Gnosis can be defined as an esoteric wisdom based on the quest for the sources of secret knowledge that can effect personal salvation or reformation of the world; while *convivència* refers to the complex realities and ideals of cultural pluralism, religious tolerance, political enlightenment, artistic renaissance, and intellectual syncretism that historically developed within Iberia, and also Sicily, as a result of the dynamic, open interaction over the centuries of Christians, Muslims, and Jews.

Given the centrality of cultural interpretation in the new history/-historicism, new medievalism, and what can be termed the new Catalanism, it is important to begin with Racionero Grau's own development of a critical and imaginative interest in the thirteenth century; this also calls for brief comparisons between the author's two historical novels *Raimon* and *Cercamón* and for mention of general parallels with Umberto Eco's historical fiction. The discussion of the postmodern use that Racionero Grau makes of the Catalan Middle Ages in general and of Llull in particular can then be put into historicist perspective by focusing on key passages that show: the cultural contexts of Mediterranean and Iberian *convivència*; the radical textuality of the gnostic traditions in the thirteenth century; Llull's quest and mission as heroic and antiheroic forms of historical narrative; the emergence of Llull's gnosis as a utopian vision; and the parallel emergence of his contemporary Arnau de Vilanova's prophecies as apocalyptic history. By way of conclusion, it is useful to describe the other Middle Ages and the other Llull that serve as points of convergence in Racionero Grau's postmodern myth and critique of Mediterranean history; for they are also part of the culturally and intellectually diverse heritage of Western Europe as it approaches the third millennium.

II. Racionero Grau's conversion to neo-Catalanism and neomedievalism.
What heightens Racionero Grau's interest in Llull is the spectacular rise, after the death of Franco (1975), of Catalan political autonomy, cultural expression, and historical revision. It is an exterior development that corresponds to the author's own inner evolution in this period. Born in the Catalan Pyrenees heartland of the Seu d'Urgell in 1940 and growing up under Franco's suppression of the Catalan cultural identity, he underwent a professional and intellectual conversion in the first decade after Franco that took him from being a civil engineer and urban planner, educated in Barcelona and Berkeley, to becoming a free-lance writer on both contemporary and esoteric themes and finally a full-fledged, widely-read historical novelist (who typically includes fifteen-page appendices on sources of and studies on the Catalan medieval renaissance). As historical novelist he is both committed to dramatizing the human encounter of new and old ideas and obsessed with the other medieval tradition of Catalonia and Occitania, which is seen to evolve outside of, or even in conflict with, the main streams of authority, orthodoxy, and hegemony of the European Christian institutions and states that emerge in the later Middle Ages and the Renaissance.

The post-Franco phenomenon of Catalan resurgence coincides with the reemergence of European local cultures and the proclamation of a postmodernist intellectual era: on the one hand, the ethnic identities and heritages of the "other Europeans" without states has been reaffirmed from Galicia in the Spain of the *autonomías* to the so-called republics of the former Yugoslavia and the former Soviet Union (now Commonwealth of Independent States); on the other hand, the disintegration of modern positivist and formalist ideologies in theory, scholarship, and the arts has led to a return to cultural historicism and philosophical hermeneutics as practiced by Bakhtin, Jauss, Foucault, and Ricoeur. It is by no means an accident, then, that Racionero Grau publishes his historical novels about supposedly heterodox figures, the troubadour Cercamón and the "illuminated doctor" Llull, in 1982 and 1985, a few years after Franco's death and the proclamation of Catalan autonomy: the first, divided in two parts, deals with the monastic renaissance in the Catalan Pyrenees in the period around 1000 and with the suppression of the Cathars during the Albigensian crusade of 1209-29; the second, which focuses on Llull's life and times, also covers other framing periods (such as Ibn Hazm's al-Andalus and even Columbus' future discoveries) and extends considerably beyond Mallorca and the Mediterranean to include China (Marco Polo) and Iran (the assassins). Racionero Grau's works appear in between the two historical romances written by Umberto Eco, the noted semiotician and medievalist (interpreter of Aquinas' esthetics), who develops his own forms of historicist revision in *The Name of the Rose* (1980) and *Foucault's Pendulum* (1988), both of which deal with the issues of late-medieval Mediterranean gnosis that so attract Racionero Grau: Eco describes marginal figures (medieval and postmodern intellectuals) engaged in the quest for ancient traditions of truth and wisdom (apostolic-mystical or gnostic-cabalistic) and associated with heterodox groups (Spiritual Franciscans and Templars), who are forced to go underground during the persecutions by church and state that unfold in the fourteenth and subsequent centuries.

III. Racionero Grau's representation of Llull's gnostic quest.
In the very title of *Raimon o el seny fantàstic*, which could be translated

as *Raimon or the Imaginative Intelligence,* Racionero Grau develops the central image of paradox and enigma in the life of the protagonist, as well as the dialectic interaction of personality and ideology in the cultural, political, and intellectual developments of his times. In order to consider the inherent possibilities and problems posed by such a novelistic approach to biography and history, it would be necessary to trace the evolution of character, theme, and image throughout the novel. This can be done in an abridged way by focusing on certain passages that summarize the author's understanding of Llull's and the thirteenth century's significance in history, but in particular in the present for Catalans.

Starting with the author's appendix as the point of departure for interpreting the composition and reception of the work, it is immediately apparent that Racionero Grau does not have any hidden agenda. On the contrary, as readers of his earlier historical novel *Cercamón* by now expect, he is quite explicit in stating his motivation for rewriting certain history as an exemplary and cautionary story: he favors historical partisanship (pro-convivència and anti-absolutist) and historiographic revision (imaginative, esoteric reconstruction vs. official, conventional traditions). This explains his interest in the cultural hybridization and intellectual syncretism represented in a historical and also emblematic manner by Llull and some of his brilliant contemporaries:

> T[omás] i J[oaquín] Carreras Artau anomenan la filosofia de Llull filosofia de frontera[:] aprofitava coneixements de la gent amb qui dialogava per utilitzar-los en argumentació (RSF notes: 276).

What is more, he focuses on a period of crisis in which a unique Iberian civilization is about to change according to the more typical patterns of uniformity, conformity, and even repression that are now being imposed from France (the centralized, absolutist state) and Rome (the hierarchical, inquisitorial papacy):

> He volgut plasmar el moment en què les tres cultures (islàmica, jueva i cristiana) coexistien en els regnes de Jaume I i els seus fills, tractant de palesar com per la intransigència de papat i dominicans aquest fet quedà ofegat, cosa que empobrí nostre país culturalment i econòmicament (RSF notes: 280).

Such a focus on a period of crisis and transformation, or for him deformation, in effect leads him to describe a temporal frontier that delimits the enlightened present about to become past (the thirteenth century with its living heritage going back to the tenth century) from the benighted future about to become present (the fourteenth century that will lead on inexorably to the twentieth). Indeed, it is this sharp focus on the fifty years from 1263 to 1313 (from the disputation of Jews and Christians in Barcelona to the suppression of the Templars in France and the rest of Europe) that distinguish the author's second historical novel from his first: in *Cercamón* the narrative, as a two-part contrastive history, jumped from the formative medieval renaissance around the year 1000 in the Catalan Pyrenees to the deformative age of national hegemony and religious persecution of the Albigensian crusade in 1209-29.

Within this general yet precise focus on a critical period, Racionero Grau focuses further on a group of four intellectuals who are all representative of their time yet marginal to the structures of power. Their intellectual acumen, the product of the Iberian *convivència*, evolves as a form of gnosis that seems to offer mystical as well as political power, since it involves the revolutionary, explosive impact of new knowledge based on ancient secret traditions and lost heterodox texts (identified by the author in the appendix [285] with the Nag Hamaddi gnostic writings found in Egypt in 1945: "he suposat que els manuscrits aplegats per Llull foren enterrats a Nag Hammadi per tal de ser revelats 'casualment' a la nostra època"). Taking several liberties as author of historical fiction (acknowledged and justified in the appendix [284]), Racionero Grau violates strict historical chronology so as to make Llull coincide and even encounter the three wise men who represent the three cultures of the Iberian medieval renaissance and who will guide him in his quest: the Hispano-Jew Abraham Nahmanides or Bonastruc de Porta (1195-1270), the Hispano-Arab Mohidin Ibn 'Arabî (1165-1240), and the Catalan Christian physician and apocalyptic writer Arnau de Vilanova (1240-1311). As the character of Ibn 'Arabî explains in the novel,

> Nosaltres estem aplegant els fragments d'una fe perduda, d'un llibre primordial perdut i retrobat, refet i dispersat, que podria unificar les religions en una metafísica universal, mostrant com totes tres...sortiren d'un mateix text, on se separaren i per què. La revelació d'això... podria canviar el curs de la història i obrir una era de concòrdia (RSF c 9: 59).

In the imagination of Racionero Grau, all four collaborate in the gnostic cause, create an elaborate network of contacts (including Cabalists, Sufis, Templars, cartographers, assassins, almogavars, merchants like Marco Polo and poets like Dante), secure a formidable collection of apocryphal and proscribed texts, and conspire to insure their ultimate vindication, if not in their problematic age, then in some more enlightened future (like the postmodern and post-Franco 1980s, the author seems to imply). For, underlying all the rhetorical trappings of esoterica, the reader finds the leitmotif of a promised age and enlightened culture, already revealed in history various times, that need only to be revived by those who are faithful to their example. Racionero Grau characterizes the sages that serve as mentors to Llull in a way that stresses their common utopian vision:

> Volien una religió que fos un pensament i una moral de tolerància per a tota la Mediterrània. Ells tres representaven el desig in-

exhaurit de tres religions que podien ser una, car totes arriben per la gnosi al mateix coneixement (RSF c 44: 247).

Human community through mystical communion, intellectual openness, and cultural tolerance is the message that is repeatedly dramatized by this confraternity and symbolized in their writings.

Beyond the cause shared by this privileged group of seers, the author develops the central narrative thread of Raimon's own discovery of that gnostic truth and his self-discovery as one called to its relentless pursuit. The most fascinating aspect of the novel is the psychological analysis of Llull's multiple influences, varied circumstances, and complex motivation. This depiction of character often takes the form of revealing monologues that show the inner struggle that accompany the outer persistence in the fulfillment of his gnostic mission:

> Volia realment convertir infidels? O anava a discutir amb ells per convèncer-se a si mateix, o per aprendre, o com a emissari polític, o com a espia? Possiblement tot alhora, i ni ell mateix se n'adonava, manipulat simultàniament per uns i altres. La seva vida era un corrent de diversos afluents polítics, religiosos i científics.... (RSF c 34: 187-88).

In what is one of the narrative strengths of the novel, Racionero Grau repeatedly draws upon Llull's own writings, both didactic and autobiographical, to give a more authentic shape to Raimon's ideals and projects as well as to illustrate the medieval writer's own perception, interiorization, and resolution of crises during his long and momentous life. This occurs in particular in reference to the poems of disillusionment and reaffirmation penned by Llull between his sixtieth and seventieth years. As part of a final sequence of soul-searching monologues, Raimon asks himself:

> Qui sóc jo? L'ombra d'un somni, un intermediari, un titella que

existeix com a joguina dels altres: vaig i vinc, porto missatges, intrigo i, endebades, penso per mi mateix; però no sé qui sóc, car em mou la llum. Sóc un emissari d'altres que, ells sí, estan quiets, segurs, impertorbats, i no cerquen. Sóc una joguina dels forts, sageta d'arcs poderosos...: viatjo, parlo i connecto què sé jo? Qui sóc jo? (RSF c 49: 263).

Such a key passage in the novel owes much of its insight and force-fulness to Llull's own *Desconhort* and *Cant de Ramon* (1295-1300). But it is Racionero Grau himself who masterfully interweaves the private with the public quest in order to show just what is at stake, in the human exchange of values and experiences, for those who pursue the wisdom of the gnostics against all historical odds and political obstacles. In this way, which is characteristically postmodern, the author plays with the heroic and antiheroic motivations, as well as cultural and psychoanalyti-cal interpretations, of the individual actor and conscience caught in the changing stream of history.

Whenever he goes back and forth from Raimon's inner struggle to the larger picture of history, of thirteenth-century Iberia and the gnostics, Racionero Grau continuously develops the opposing terms of the signs of things and the signs of the times. Indeed, he even makes Llull a representative of the first, a type of understanding of a gnostic intrahistory, and Arnau a spokesman for the second, a form of expres-sion of a conspiratorial *Realpolitik* turned into apocalyptic prophecy. For Llull, the pursuit of the signs of things is manifest in his public life as the point of departure for an enlightened utopia ruled perhaps by philosopher kings like Prester John or Llull's own pope Blanquerna. both of which are mentioned in the novel (178 and 192-93). Apparently, as he informs one of his Cistercian friends at the monastery of the Real in Mallorca, those visionaries and systematizers who preceded him were not utopian enough:

> --[A]ltres abans que vós han cregut descobrir la ciéncia univer-
> sal.... --[N]ingú no l'ha explicada sencera com ara jo estic dispo-
> sat a fer.
> --Què penseu assolir...?
> --La concòrdia de tots els homes en una mateixa religió i mateixa
> ciència, ja que tots tindran un mateix sistema de pensar (RSF c
> 14: 80).

However, there is another more private, and ultimately problematic, side to this gnostic pursuit of truth in the thing itself: the isolation it can bring from the historical moment and its call to action. Racionero Grau gives the reader a telling portrait that epitomizes the contemplative and gnostic sage absorbed in the transformative and fruitful meditations that he undertakes in Mallorca:

> Lluny de fam, de feina i de neguit, Llull seguia a Randa els seus
> somnis de veritat i ciència.... Aliè als ombrívols signes dels
> temps, Raimon estava immers fins al moll dels ossos en els signes
> de les coses (RSF c 15: 86).

Although Racionero Grau does show Llull's concern with the impact of his gnosis on society and history, it appears as a general utopian sentiment, albeit expressed in strenuous travels and decisive encounters with men of influence, which does not approach the pragmatic utopian model of Llull's own novel *Blanquerna*. Nevertheless, in Racionero Grau's recreation of the historical episode of Raimon's founding of the missionary school of Miramar, he does strike a partial balance in favor of the visionary as responsible man of action. The benefits to others, as well as to the gnostics, of a world ruled by tolerance and harmony are here described in an all-inclusive wave of optimism:

> Com voldria jo un món subtil, alegre, refinat..., un món clar i net
> on la gent treballin amb repòs, parlin calmosament i somriguin.
> Viatjar pertot arreu entre amics: àrabs, cristians, jueus, ben rebut
> a tot arreu, a casa en qualsevulga ciutat del món (RSF c 34: 185).

Indeed, this passage summarizes what does take place in the novel when Nahmanides, Ibn 'Arabî, and Arnau all converge on Miramar to share their knowledge and vision with Llull and his disciples. But the last image the author gives of Llull is in fact that of the gnostic visionary:

> El sol eixia com un tercer ull de foc al front de l'horitzó, entre les parpelles del mar i l'òrbita del cel.... Raimon es girà vers la llum i adorà el rei del món, l'ull (RSF c 51: 271).

The elaborate image, narratologically satisfying but ideologically problematic, of Llull contemplating himself as he contemplates the truth of things in nature and in God, is symbolized by the metaphor of the solar and mystical eye (*l'ull*), which in the original Catalan, when read aloud, serves as a pun on Llull's own name. Thus the concentric hermetic circles of microcosm and macrocosm, as well as of perception and self-perception, are recapitulated in a striking image that nevertheless takes the reader out of the historical narrative and cultural context of the novel into the closest approximation that Racionero Grau can create of Lullian utopia as a gnostic uchronia: this emerges as a self-reflective state of knowing and being that lies outside of the vicissitudes of time and manifests itself beyond the discourse of history. Yet, ironically, what makes this state possible, as Racionero makes clear throughout the novel, is Llull's lifelong experience of the unique moment of Iberian *convivèn-cia* which he has been privileged to know and embrace

IV. Racionero Grau's interpretation of Arnau's apocalyptic prophecy.

In Racionero Grau's revisionist approach to the thirteenth century, which cannot all be encompassed in the "secret biography" of Llull, it is left to Arnau de Vilanova to embody the gnostics' prophetic judgment on history and to articulate the reformers' apocalyptic reading of the signs of the times. True to life, as witnessed by his surviving texts ("Confessió de Barcelona," "Lliçó de Narbona," "Raonament d'Avinyó," "Informació espiritual," 1305-1310), from which the author draws for key speeches in the novel, Arnau offers at one point a revealing explanation of his motives in employing the paradoxically historical/ahistorical discourse of prophecy and apocalypse:

> Quan parlo de la fi del món, parlo del món que nosaltres hem conegut, on regnava la tolerància religiosa i l'afany de saber. Ara aneu cap a un món dogmàtic, restrictiu, on l'única prova admesa és la raó.... L'Anticrist és el cos místic dels negadors, simoníacs, dogmàtics i inquisidors (RSF c 32: 176).

Echoing the outlook and language of such late-medieval visionaries as the Joachimites and Spiritual Franciscans, who are all mentioned in the novel (RSF 173, 192-95, 201, 222), Arnau in effect fuses contemporary movements for the reform of church and society with the idealist utopian or mystical visions of various eccentric and heterodox figures of his age.

The inner light of gnosis and outer thunderbolt of protest serve to emphasize by contrast the new dark ages that will cover Europe as church and state turn their back on the culturally pluralistic and ideologically syncretist medieval renaissances of al-Andalus, Occitania, Catalonia, and Sicily:

> Una tenebra baixarà sobre aquest segle: els quatre genets, la pesta, la fam, la guerra i la mort, el devastaran. Morirà l'esperit que l'animava i creuran en un fugisser renaixement que portarà a més guerra i intolerància.... (RSF c 44: 248).

What will emerge in place of the medieval *convivència* and gnosis, are the late-scholastic and humanist utopias, which lead to the social dystopia and political anti-utopia of the Renaissance and Reformation. For the author these represent far more limited, uniform, and grimmer, periods that will beget the totalitarian states and mechanical mentalities of the twentieth century:

> [P]assarà una època negra en què la matèria imposi el regne de la quantitat. Voldran saber-ho tot i fruiran del poder mecànic de la ciència, però es trobaran sols i cecs davant l'univers immens i mut.... [S]eran poderosos, i faran poderosos disbarats. Fins que arribi la fi del regne de la Bèstia; aleshores nosaltres podrem recomençar (RSF c 44: 248).

In typically postmodernist, neohistoricist manner, Racionero Grau makes use of Arnau's prophetic works to show a self-awareness among medieval gnostics of their historical role: theirs proves to be a critical period that only becomes recognizable as such precisely when it is perceived to be already in the process of declining or rather falling under another age in which their models and discourses will be totally suppressed. But when still other ages emerge to redress the balance and review alternative versions of the past, then what was once only historical contrast and ideological difference can be transformed into transhistorical continuity and crosscultural sympathy.

Ultimately, as the novel shows in dramatic and prophetic terms, it is a question of competing late-medieval systems of summas and utopias coming to a historically decisive confrontation. The mystical and apostolic utopia of the Cathars, Cabalists, Sufis, Joachimites, Templars, and Spirituals is defeated in the public acts of history by the forces of law and order (the absolutist French monarchy and Rome-Avignon papacy) who seek to impose their own utopia of orthodoxy (Thomas Aquinas), conformity (Inquisition), and hegemony (Christian nation-states). Yet the latter cannot overcome the former within the secret traditions of history (a gnostic intrahistory) that serve to preserve ancient archetypes, alternate ideals, apocryphal myths, exemplary lives, and extracanonical texts until they can be rediscovered, recognized, and reinterpreted by new sages in future ages of enlightenment. In fact, the author's judgment is supported by Llull scholars (cf. Colomer, Gandillac, and Yates) who have studied the Mallorcan thinker's impact on major Renaissance humanists, such as Giordano Bruno, Nicholas de Cusa, and Giovanni Pico della Mirandola, who were known for their gnostic, syncretist, heterodox, radical, and reformist positions. Llull's and his fellow gnostics and reformers' utopia is shown by Racionero Grau to be more open in intellect, more enlightened in politics, more spiritual in religion, and more tolerant in ethics than that of their rivals, persecutors, and successors. That is why it survived so long in the minds, imaginations, and hearts of Catalans and others, until now it can at last be acknowledged as a fitting model in the present generation's search for a renewed convivència and a humane gnosis.

V. Theoretical conclusions: The other Middle Ages.

If, as it is claimed in this study, the appearance of Racionero Grau's historical novel on Ramon Llull corresponds to a series of cultural and intellectual phenomena that can all be included under the umbrella terms of neohistoricism and neomedievalism, then it is crucial to establish just what form of new interpretations of thirteenth-century Catalan *convivèn-cia* and gnosis are being represented. In essence, it can be said that Racionero Grau writes about the other Llull, as the gnostic-mystic sage, and the other Late Middle Ages, as the heterogeneous and heterodox age of Cathars and Spirituals, because for him, as for many postmodernist intellectuals, the alterity of the distant past serves to break with the familiarity of the recent past and symbolize the alterity/familiarity of a future that promises to return to overall continuities in the human search for wisdom based on the reasonable and humane (as well as mysterious and spiritual) understanding of common experience. The author's ideological motivation in dealing with Catalan history betrays the cultural relativism that is involved in using the terms alterity/familiarity and medieval/modern/postmodern.

This relativism is precisely the major critical point made in the self-conscious hermeneutics offered by neohistoricism. As Burke observes: "The philosophical foundation of the new history is the idea that reality is socially or culturally constituted" (3). Veeser adds that the new historicism focuses on "selves and texts [that] are defined by their relation to hostile others...and disciplinary power" (xiii); indeed, "it encourages us to admire the sheer intricacy and unavoidability of exchanges between culture and power" (xi). It is thus significant that Racionero Grau privileges a period that for him represents the last flowering of enlightened heterodoxy before the imposition by church and state of a totalitarian conformity to established authority: as is hinted in one passage in the novel uttered by Arnau de Vilanova (RSF 248), this will culminate in the excesses of both the Protestant Reformation and the Catholic Counter Reformation and will extend to twentieth-century manifestations of a rationalist, absolutist, and inquisitorial mentality that bases power on social and religious conformity.

Such an interpretation is not only ideologically motivated but also culturally defined. For as the on-going revision of medieval religious history makes clear, the phenomenology of heresy is fundamental to understanding the forms of authority and even discourse developed by the establishment in its cultural dialogue and ideological dialectic with the margins of society, the frontiers of civilizations, and the limits of human thought. In this light, it should be stressed that contemporary scholars go even further than Racionero Grau in their revisionist history of thirteenth-century heterodoxy and heresy: Lambert points to the development of symbiotic relations between religious and secular forces both within and in reaction to the Cathar communities of southern France (392); Russell emphasizes the social rhetoric of orthodox attacks on marginal groups that leads to the evolution of absolutism and alterity in the self-definition of the dominant groups (61-62); and Ozment underscores the paradox that the orthodox response of Thomas Aquinas' synthesis of faith and reason led to the escalation of conflicts between church and state for total control of the hearts, minds, bodies, and souls of European Christians (20).

What Racionero Grau actually attempts to do and in fact succeeds in doing—bringing to novelistic life the history of late-medieval cultures, personalities, and ideas engaged in the struggle for knowledge and power in the Western Mediterranean—should be distinguished on the level of textuality from what neohistoricist and neomedievalist critics do in their theory and scholarship. Yet it still bears a close resemblance on the level of context and pretext to the latter's key strategy of interpretation as a dialogic process of comparative and self-critical evaluation. As Cantor explains:

> Medieval civilization stands toward our postmodern culture as the conjunctive other, the intriguing shadow, the marginally distinctive double, the secret sharer of our dreams and anxieties.... [T]he Middle Ages are much like the culture of today, but exhibit just enough variations to disturb us and force us to question some of our values and behavior patterns and to propose some alternatives or at least modifications. The difference is relatively small, but all the more provocative for that (47).

The focus of discussion shared by Racionero Grau and the neohistoricists involves the interplay of historical experiences as cultural discourses about identity and community, authority and power. The author's provocative insights on Llull and the thirteenth century are designed to challenge the postmodern Catalan reader to compare and revise his own formative histories and stories.

Such a fascination with late-medieval mentality as a textuality/-contextuality that offers a historically decisive and culturally exemplary model for the present is ultimately reinforced by one of the deans of medievalists, Paul Zumthor, who is himself a convert to neomedievalism. It is with Zumthor's words that I should like to conclude:

> "The Middle Ages created, from heterogeneous elements, the [cultural and intellectual] languages we speak today. It forged most of the discourses that we use and that give form to our instincts and thoughts. This has been said for a long time now...about our discourse of love. It ought to be said [also] about our political, even economic, discourse, and the multiple forms of... 'canonical discourse,' which claims that everything human may be encompassed by science and the law" (13).

As Racionero Grau perceptively shows, it was Llull's destiny to be drawn into the thirteenth-century dialectic on the discourses of gnosis or science and the law, of hermetic knowledge and worldly politics, but it was his genius that led him to recognize the new power of such discourses and it was his passionate vision that enabled him at times to transcend them in a spirit of Iberian and Mediterranean *convivència*.

Dept. of Modern Languages and Literatures
The Catholic University of America
Washington, DC 20064

Works Cited or Consulted

A. Text studied

RSF = Racionero Grau, Lluís. *Raimon o el seny fantàstic*. Barcelona: Laia, 1985.

B. Other texts

Eco, Umberto. *Foucault's Pendulum. Tr. W. Weaver. New York:*

Random House, Ballantine, 1990. [Orig.: Il pendolo de Foucault. Milan: Bompiani, 1988.]

---. The Name of the Rose. San Diego: Harcourt Brace Jovanovich,
1983. [Orig.: Il nome della rosa. Milan: Bompiani, 1980.]

Llull, Ramon. Arbre de sciència. In Obres essencials. Barcelona:
Selecta, 1957, vol. 1: 555-1040.

---. [Blanquerna =] Libre de Evast e Blanquerna. 4 vols. Eds. S.
Galmés, A. Caimari, R. Guilleumas. Barcelona: Barcino, 1935,
1947, 1954.

---. Cant de Ramon and Desconhort. In Poesies. Ed. R. Alòs-
Moner. Barcelona: Barcino, 1928: 30-33 and 65-105.

---. Libre d'Amic e Amat. Eds. M. Olivar, S. Galmés [1927]. Barcelona:
Barcino, 1980, 2nd ed.

---. Obres essencials. 2 vols. Eds. M. Batllori, T. and J. Carreras
Artau, J. Rubió Balaguer, et al. Barcelona: Selecta, 1957-60.

---. Phantasticus (Disputa del clergue Pere i de Ramon, el Fantàstic). Tr.-ed. L. Badia. Barcelona: Stelle dell'Orsa, 1985.

---. Vida coètania. In Obres Essencials. Barcelona: Selecta, 1957,
vol. 1: 31-54.

Racionero Grau, Lluís. Cercamón [novel on Catalonia-Occitania, 10th-
13th centuries]. Barcelona: Edicions 62, 1982.

---. Filosofías del undergound. Barcelona: Anagrama, 1977.

---. La Mediterrània i els bàrbars del Nord. Barcelona: Laia, 1985.

---. Vilanova, Arnau de. "Confessió de Barcelona," "Lliçó de Narbo
na," "Raonament d'Avinyó," and "Informació espiritual al rei
Frederic [III]." In Obres catalanes, vol. 1: Escrits religiosos. Ed.

M. Batllori. Barcelona: Barcino, 1947.

C. Fiction and legend about Llull

Frère, Jean-Claude. *Raymond Lulle: Le docteur illuminé.* Paris: Grasset, 1972.

Graux, Lucien. *Le Docteur illuminé* [novel]. Paris: Fayard, 1927.

Llompart, Gabriel. "La leyenda del desengaño en la conversión de Llull." *Analecta Sacra Tarraconiensia* 36 (1963): 283-98.

Nollier, Inès. *Le Magicien de Montpellier: Raymond Lulle* [novel]. Mesnil-sur-l'Estrée: Rocher, 1990.

Waite, Arthur E. "Raymund Lully." In *Three Famous Alchemists.* Philadelphia: David McKay, 1900.

D. Studies on Llull

Bonner, Anthony. "Introduction." *Selected Works of Ramon Llull.* Princeton: Princeton U.P., 1985: 3-89.

Bonner, Anthony and Lola Badia. *Ramon Llull: Vida, pensament i obra literària.* Barcelona: Empúries, 1988.

Carreras Artau, Tomás y Joaquín. *Historia de filosofía española: Filosofía cristiana de los siglos XIII al XV.* 2 vols. Madrid: Real Acad. CEFN, 1939-43.

Cohen, Jeremy. "Raymond Lull" *The Friars and Jews: Evolution of Medieval Anti-Semitism.* Ithaca: Cornell U.P., 1982: 199-226.

Colomer, Eusebio. *De la Edad Media al Renacimiento: Ramon Llull, Nicolás de Cusa, Juan Pico della Mirandola.* Barcelona: Herder, 1975.

---. "El pensament ecumènic de Ramon Llull." *Estudis de llengua i literatura catalanes oferts a R. Aramon Serra*. Barcelona: Curial, 1983, vol. 3: 61-80.

Cruz Hernández, Miguel. *El pensamiento de Ramon Llull*. Valencia: Castalia, Fundación Juan March, 1977.

Gandillac, Maurice de. "De quelques utopies (ou semi-utopie) de la concorde universelle: Abelard, Lulle, Nicolas de Cuse, Postel, Campanella." *Studies in Honour of Ferran Valls Taberner*, 9: 2583-98. Barcelona: PPU, 1989.

Garcías Palou, Sebastián. *Ramon Llull en la historia del ecumenismo*. Barcelona: Herder, 1986.

---. *Ramon Llull y el Islam*. Madrid: Gráficas Planisi, 1981.

González-Casanovas, Roberto J. "Ramon Llull, Popular Religious Fiction, and Cultural Historicism." *Proceedings of the First Catalan Symposium*. Ed. J. M. Solà-Solé. New York: P e t e r Lang, 1992: 57-70.

Greive, Herman. "Ramon Llull und die Kabbala." *Freiburger Z. für Philosophie und Theologie* 20 (1973): 324-31. [Tr.: "Ramon Llull i la càbala" *Calls* 3 (1988-89): 75-82.]

Kedar, Benjamin. "The Many Opinions of Ramon Llull." *Crusade and Mission: European Approaches toward the Muslims*. Princeton U.P., 1982: 189-99.

Meddeb, Abdelwahab. "La religión del otro: Ibn 'Arabí/Llull." *Cruce de culturas y mestizaje cultural*. Ed. T. Todorov. Madrid: Júcar, 1988: 131-44.

Menocal, María Rosa. "Love and Mercy at the Edge of Madness: Ramon Llull's *Book of the Lover and Beloved* and Ibn 'Arabî's 'O doves of the arâk and the bân trees...'" *Catalan Review* 4, 1-2 (1990): 155-77.

Pereira, Michaela. *The Alchemical Works Attributed to Raymond Lull.* London: Warburg Inst., 1989.

---. "La leggenda di Lullo alchimista." *Estudios Lulianos* 27, 2 (1987): 145-63.

---. "Lullian Alchemy: Aspects and Problems of the *Corpus* of Alchemical Works Attributed to Ramon Llull (XIV-XVII Centuries)." *Catalan Review* 4, 1-2 (1990): 41-54.

Raymond Lulle: Christianisme, Judaïsme, Islam [Colloquium, Fribourg 1984]. Ed. R. Imbach. Fribourg: Éd. Universitaires, 1986.

Raymond Lulle et le pays d'Oc. Ed. M.-H. Vicaire. *Cahiers de Fanjeaux* 22. Toulouse: Privat, 1987.

Romano, David. "Llull e la cultura ebraica." *Annali Istituto Universitario Orientale di Napoli, Sezione Romanze* 34, 1 (1992): 171-89.

Satz, Mario. "Raymond Lulle et la Kabbale." In *Raymond Lulle: Christianisme, Judaïsme, Islam.* Ed. R. Imbach. Fribourg: Éd. Universitaires, 1986: 59-69.

Urvoy, Dominique. *Penser l'Islam: Les présupposés islamiques de l'"Art" de Lull.* Paris: J. Vrin, 1980.

---. "La place de Ramon Llull dans la pensée arabe." *Catalan Review* 4, 1-2 (1990): 201-220.

Yates, Frances A. *Lull and Bruno.* London: Routledge, 1982.

E. Historical Background

Alomar, Gabriel. *Cátaros y occitanos en el reino de Mallorca.* Palma de Mallorca: Luis Ripoll, 1978.

Burckhardt, Titus. *El esoterismo islámico.* Madrid: Taurus, 1980.

Chiat, Marilyn and Kathryn Reyerson, eds. *The Medieval Mediterra nean: Crosscultural Contacts*. St.   Cloud,   Minn.:   North Star, 1988.

El debat intercultural als segles XIII i XIV [Colloquium, Gerona 1988]. Ed. M. Salleras. *Estudi General* 9 (1989).

Gurevich, Aron J. *Medieval Popular Culture: Problems of Belief and Perception*. Trs. J. M. Bak and P. A. Hollingsworth. Cambridge: Cambridge U.P., 1988.

Hillgarth, J. N. "Mallorca como centro intelectual, 1229-1550." *Anuario de Estudios Medievales* 19 (1989): 205-11.

Lambert, Malcom. *Medieval Heresy: Popular Movements from the Gregorian Reform to the Reformation*. Oxford: Blackwell, 1992, 2nd ed.

Monroe, James T. *Islam and the Arabs in Spanish Scholarship*. Leiden: E. J. Brill, 1970.

Ozment, Steven. *The Age of Reform, 1250-1550: An Intellectual and Religious History of Late Medieval and Reformation Europe*. New Haven: Yale U.P., 1980.

Russell, Jeffrey B. *Dissent and Order in the Middle Ages: The Search for Legitimate Authority*. New York: Twayne, 1992.

Simon, Larry J. *Society and Religion in the Kingdom of Majorca, 1229-c. 1300*. Ph.D. dissertation, UCLA 1989.

F. Critical Theory and New Medievalism

Brownlee, Kevin, Marina S. Brownlee, Stephen G. Nichols, eds. *The New Medievalism*. Baltimore: Johns Hopkins U.P., 1991.

Burke, Peter, ed. *New Perspectives on Historical Writing*. University Park: Pennsylvania St. U.P., 1992.

Cantor, Norman F. *Inventing the Middle Ages: The Lives, Works, and Ideas of the Great Medievalists of the Twentieth Century.* New York: W. Morrow, 1991.

Foucault, Michel. *The Archeology of Knowledge and the Discourse on Language.* Tr. A. M. S. Smith. New York: Pantheon, 1972.

González-Casanovas, Roberto J. "Text and Context in Alfonsine Studies: Is the New Medievalism for Alfonsistas?" *Exemplaria Hispanica* 1 (1991-92): vii-xxxiv.

Grumley, John E. *History and Totality: Radical Historicism from Hegel to Foucault.* London: Routledge, 1989.

Jauss, Hans Robert. *Toward an Aesthetic of Reception.* Tr. T. Bahti. Minneapolis: U. of Minnesota P., 1982.

Jauss, Hans Robert et al. *Medieval Literature and Contemporary Theory. New Literary History* 10, 2 (1979): 181-416.

Ricoeur, Paul. *Hermeneutics and the Human Sciences: Essays on Language, Action, and Interpretation.* Ed. J. B. Thompson. Cambridge: Cambridge U.P., 1981.

Veeser, H. Aram, ed. *The New Historicism.* New York: Routledge, 1989.

White, Hayden. *The Content of the Form: Narrative Discourse and Historical Representation.* Baltimore: Johns Hopkins U.P., 1987.

Zumthor, Paul. *Speaking of the Middle Ages.* Tr. S. White. Lincoln: U. of Nebraska P., 1986. [Orig.: *Parler du Moyen Âge.* Paris: Minuit, 1980.]

Maria Guasch

IMATGES DE LA MATERNITAT A
QUILÒMETRES DE TUL PER A UN PETIT CADÀVER D'ANTÒNIA VICENS

L'univers narratiu d'Antònia Vicens està poblat de figures femenines que qüestionen constantment l'espai que l'estructuració patriarcal del món els ha permès ocupar i lluiten per superar-ne els límits, lluita que desemboca sovint en la follia com a única resolució de conflictes poderosos que les imposicions ideològiques i socials fan difícils, o impossibles, de resoldre. A *Quilòmetres de tul per a un petit cadàver* aquests conflictes giren al voltant de la institució de la maternitat, creant una tensió entre el paper de mare, tal com està socialment determinat i controlat, i la necessitat de transcendir-lo perquè pugui emergir l'ésser integral de la dona com a persona.

Maria, la narradora i protagonista de *Quilòmetres*, s'embarca en un procés de transgressió del paper de mare tal com el planteja el seu context social i ideològic, context caracteritzat per una definició masculina de l'espai femení en funció de la capacitat reproductora de la dona, i que li exigeix la renúncia a qualsevol altra de les possibilitats que ajuden a la realització personal dels éssers humans. En relació amb aquesta definició, que sol anomenar-se, amb el terme de Betty Friedan, com a "mística de la feminitat,"[1] és important ressaltar la distinció d'Adrienne Rich entre la maternitat com a experiència (la relació potencial de la dona amb els fills i amb el seu poder de reproducció) i com a institució que vol assegurar que aquest potencial es mantingui sota el poder masculí.[2]

La transgressió de la narradora, que consisteix en una problematització de la definició de la dona com a renúncia al seu desig, es reflexa en l'escriptura del diari que constitueix la novel·la: "faig aquesta mena de diari, aquesta mena de delicte, ja que escric d'amagat, com a únic acte propi."[3] La marca del "delicte" és la voluntat d'auto-coneixement com a primer pas per superar la supeditació al desig de l'Altre i arribar a una autodefinició compatible amb el propi desig. Malgrat que el diari s'estructura al voltant de dates que corresponen, la majoria, a visites al psiquiatra, la narració no reprodueix el contingut de les consultes sinó que, independentment d'aquestes, esdevé l'instrument que permet l'autoexploració que el diàleg amb l'analista no arriba a propiciar. Malgrat que "les paraules normalment em fugen a l'hora d'intentar contar, descriure, el més íntim, essencial, acostat a mi mateixa" (38), el diari és per a la narradora l'única via d'accés al "pou profundíssim" (92) del seu ésser i del seu desig:

> un navegar, un endinsar-me per les aigües secretes de l'encanteri, una passa més i em trob, i m'agaf, i em rescat, però hi ha el precipici de l'avior i en sent el vertigen... (126).

Aquest rescatar-se, arribar al fons per intentar entendre's a ella mateixa i el context en què està immersa, es revela com un exercici necessàriament solitari perquè parteix de preocupacions i inquietuds que no són compartides. D'aquí que sigui el diari, el monòleg amb ella mateixa, la forma més apropiada de dur-lo a terme degut a l'absència d'interlocutors idonis. La comunicació i el diàleg són impossibles (encara que "lo que jo voldria és comunicació, parlar" [23]), especialment amb les dues figures masculines centrals de la novel·la, el psiquiatre i el marit, perquè ambdós encarnen i defenen els condicionaments ideològics que ella busca transcendir. Quan s'estableix el diàleg, com per exemple amb la veïna, és tanmateix improductiu perquè aquesta no comparteix la necessitat de qüestionar el seu espai de dona.

El navegar "per les aigües secretes de l'encanteri" a les pàgines del diari resulta en una narració que, guiada pel "vertigen," que és una manifestació de la follia, agafa tortuosos camins que combinen els esdeveniments de la vida quotidiana amb "una escampadissa de records tèrbols" (14), i amb les imaginacions i interpretacions del "meu pensament (colometa missatgera que et perds, et perds)" (21), combinació que crea un univers regit més pel desig que per la realitat. Així, la follia és l'element textual que permet el pas del món històric i ideològic de la narradora al món simbòlic del seu discurs, ja que és el punt de partida d'un sistema d'imatges recurrents que expressen, amb profunda lucidesa, la significació humana d'una determinada situació històrica i existencial.

El discurs de la narradora s'estableix al voltant de l'experiència de la maternitat, transmesa a partir de la relació que s'estableix amb els dos fills: des de l'obsessiva dependència del petit, expressada en termes d'extrema possessió ("com que sa mamà es meva, jo mataré sa mamà" [13]), a una certa indiferència per part del major, que il·lustra el procés d'independització del fill, el pas de dependre d'ella totalment, d'anar "aferrat a ses meves faldes" (29), fins el moment en què "la besada té el fregadís fred del menyspreu, les paraules el to lleuger de la indiferència" (39). La mort simbòlica de la mare, present en l'actitud del fill petit, il·lustra com la institució de la maternitat, sota el poder masculí, anul·la i destrueix les potencialitats de la dona en funció d'una entrega total i absoluta al paper de mare, destrucció que es fa més evident amb el buit que sobrevé amb l'independència dels fills. La presència de l'anul·lació de la dona-mare com a element constant al món patriarcal permet a Luce

Irigaray afirmar que el matricidi és la base originària sobre la qual funcionen la nostra societat i la nostra cultura.[4]

La institució de la maternitat, definida com a mort de la dona, és a dir, la seva anul·lació com a persona, s'expressa a nivell discursiu a través de la interacció de dos camps metafòrics principals, la terra i l'aire, que formen un eix vertical la base del qual és el cos femení, la seva definició i la seva experiència. I la reacció dels personatges vindrà expressada per la posició que intenten ocupar en aquest eix, com veurem en el cas de la narradora i del marit.

La terra és el símbol per excel·lència de la fecunditat i, per extensió, de la maternitat, per la qual cosa és freqüentment associada amb l'element femení de l'existència; per a la narradora representa tot allò que anul·la la seva possibilitat d'autorealització. La combinació dels dos principals aspectes dels cicles naturals de la terra (la mort i la destrucció, per un costat, i la fecunditat i la renovació, per l'altre) ressalta l'aspecte negatiu de la maternitat com a institució patriarcal: l'anul·lació i la destrucció que prové d'esborrar les pròpies necessitats i les pròpies ànsies en funció d'un paper socialment determinat, que supedita la dona al interessos del "sembrador" (el marit i les institucions patriarcals). La connexió de l'aspecte creatiu de la terra amb el seu element oposat i complementari, la mort, es posa de relleu en la figura de la mare morta, recordada com a "dona estones àrida, estones flonja, talment la terra" (15). El donar vida als fills esdevé, metafòricament, la mort de la mare, i així la pròpia mort de la narradora, juganerament al·ludida pel fill petit, enllaça amb una cadena de mares mortes, de la qual la seva mare n'és la màxima exponent. La figura de la mare morta és l'únic model permès per la política sexual patriarcal, la força de la qual és aclaparadora per a la narradora que "filla de ma mare, encara no he aconseguit ésser dona" (52), i que es veu a ella mateixa, "i per tots els dies de vida…arrossegant un cadàver vestit de núvia" (80). La imatge del cadàver de la mare vestit de núvia, reforçada per la referència nupcial dels quilòmetres de tul (recordem el títol de la novel·la), al·ludeix clarament a les dues institucions, el matrimoni i la maternitat, que defineixen i regulen l'espai de la narradora, i les conseqüències de les quals són representades a la seva imaginació amb la presència constant del cadàver de la mare, que se li apareix per "veure i escoltar les petites coses familiars des d'un estri diferent, de vegades rosegó de pa, de vegades cullera" (150).

Si a nivell simbòlic la terra il·lustra el poder destructor de la maternitat com a institució socialment construïda, també a nivell literal té fortes connotacions negatives per a la narradora perquè il·lustra una vegada més la misèria de la supeditació a l'Altre: recorda la seva infantesa al camp com una època de misèria i de dificultats familiars ("el meus avis treballant la terra d'altri, ajupits de l'alba a la posta de sol, un rosegó de pa per a menjar" [126]).

En contrast, Jaume, el marit, "donaria mitja vida per tornar treballar es camp" (93), per tornar a sentir-se "identificat, integrat, segur, dins el regne inalterable de la naturalesa" (130). El pas del camp a la ciutat l'ha deixat sense base concreta per viure perquè per a ell la terra és allò que es pot posseir i controlar. Aquesta forta connexió amb la terra complementa la connexió amb la seva mare, i la desaparició de les dues (la mort de la mare i la venda de les terres) és vista com a pèrdua similar que li permet afirmar "ara no tenc res" (94). En ambdós casos en Jaume és el beneficiari de la fecunditat, tant de la terra com de la mare: les anyades que cull de la terra es complementen amb l'atenció constant que rep d'una mare que dóna prioritat a les necessitats del fill. D'aquesta combinació de mare i terra provenia la seva seguretat. L'actitud del marit coincideix amb la visió, identificada per Bachelard, de la terra com a refugi, com a retorn a la mare, com a imatge principal d'intimitat i de seguretat.[5] La narradora, en canvi, té una visió de la

terra no anticipada per Bacherlard, que es limita principalment a l'estudi
de textos masculins i no ha considerat que homes i dones poden tenir una
relació diferent amb el que ell anomena "le plus grand de tous les
archétypes, la Mère."[6] Per tant, al seu estudi no té cabuda la imatge
amb què s'expressa en aquesta novel·la la constatació de que la institució
de la maternitat "has alienated women from our bodies by incarcerating
us in them"[7]: la terra, i el cos, com a presó, imatge que es connecta
estretament amb la de la terra com a tomba per tal de suggerir amb més
força la idea de la mort simbòlica de la mare.

L'actitud contraposada de la narradora i del marit envers la
fecunditat de la terra i, per extensió, envers la maternitat i el paper social
de la dona, fa impossible la reconciliació i el diàleg. Això il·lustra
eficaçment el desequilibri que la ideologia patriarcal imposa en les
relacions home-dona, en les quals la dona és entesa únicament en funció
de la realització dels altres, mai de la seva pròpia.

L'intent d'emergir com a dona no definida únicament pel paper
de mare, és a dir, l'intent de néixer com a persona, és expressat com a
allunyament de la terra (entesa com a representació d'una definició
patriarcal del cos femení) mitjançant la metàfora de l'aire, que, coincidint
amb les conclusions de Bachelard al seu estudi de les imatges aèries,[8] és
l'element que connota la llibertat, el moviment ascendent, lliure i sense
resistència i, per tant, el món del desig. La imatge que la narradora
associa amb l'aire és la miloca, i la miloca rompuda expressa els somnis
romputs, perduts o impossibles. El desig insatisfet s'encarna nostàlgica-
ment en la figura de Miquel, amor adolescent, de clares connotacions
aèries: "Còsmic, eteri, havia d'encalçar-lo pels niguls, remuntar-me,
estendre les ales del cor, convertir-me en gavina capriciosa i explorar
l'infinit,...ell sempre un estel corredís" (144). Hi ha intents de recuperar
simbòlicament la llibertat a través de l'aire, com pujar al terrat amb el
fill petit a fer volar una miloca, intents que fracassen consistentment ("i

el vent que em va prendre el fil i se'n va dur la miloca cel enllà" [49]),
perquè l'aire és aquí l'element que permet la llibertat, però és també
intangible i inabastable com les seves ànsies.

La principal expressió simbòlica d'aquesta impossibilitat de
transcendir la terra és un embaràs imaginari que representa el poder
empresonador de la terra i que marca el fracàs del seu intent, a nivell de
la seva participació en el món social, d'alliberar-se de la definició
masculina de l'espai femení, d'enlairar-se per transcendir-lo.

Al començament de tal intent, la narradora entén la importància,
si vol arribar a "ésser, pensar en mi mateixa" (46) i sortir del camí que
el pensament masculí li ha traçat, de trencar amb la dependència,
principalment econòmica, que és la principal dificultat per posar en
pràctica el consell del seu fill gran de separar-se del marit, consell que
coincideix amb el seu desig d'explorar nous espais i noves possibilitats.
Malgrat que el món del treball li és completament estrany, està disposada
a aprofitar les limitades oportunitats que li puguin ésser accessibles
("Fregar escales, vaig dir jo, de dependenta, vaig dir jo, dec servir per
qualque cosa, vaig dir jo" [64]), i arriba a la precària solució de la venda
de desodorant. En la seva poc afortunada incursió en el món del treball,
la narradora té com a contrapunt la figura de la veïna, que també es
mostra insatisfeta, però no pel seu paper de dona definit per una societat
patriarcal, sinó per la impossibilitat d'integrar-se plenament dins aquesta
societat i aprofitar-ne els avantatges materials. La solució al seu
problema (el fet que el marit vagi a la presó la priva de la relativa
prosperitat que ell li oferia, representada per les pulseres d'or) la veu en
termes de dependència: "si fóssim dones riques, o dones guapes, com
aquestes de ses revistes, no tindríem problemes, un home ens deixaria i
un altre ens engosparia" (58).

En contrast amb la veïna, la narradora té una reacció més
complexa davant els models femenins fornits pels mitjans de comunicació

i d'entreteniment. Hi ha dues pel·lícules que li serveixen de referència i són obsessions recurrents; són dos "westerns," gènere que en la seva forma típica encarna valors racistes i sexistes i que serveix aquí per presentar dues actituds diferents de la dona davant l'agressió, ambdues insatisfactòries: Kelly amb l'acceptació voluntària de l'agressió i la metgessa amb l'autodestrucció com a única sortida ("Aquella va dir: coneixeràs sa rossa més tremenda que et puguis imaginar, i sa metgessa va dir: jes, beu, porc" [71]). No hi ha, però, un tercer model que s'ajusti a les necessitats de la narradora, un model que permeti destruir les circumstàncies opressives sense autodestruir-se al mateix temps, i la incapacitat de construir-se-la ella mateixa desemboca en la follia, entesa com a incapacitat d'establir una relació estable amb el món.[9]

Les maneres en què la narradora intuïa poder arribar en aquesta tercera via, als seus somnis de rompre amb el seu estat d'"enterrament," es demostren impossibles o ineficaces, començant pel món del treball que no ha suposat una sortida degut a que les seves potencialitats mai no han estat desenvolupades. L'altra manera era viure la llibertat desitjada a través dels fills mascles i els seus privilegis dins un món masculí ("ell [Jaumet] una continuació de mi mateixa, la part ofegada, a la fi, tenia vida pròpia, voluntat pròpia, baronívola i descarada la veu, tant de temps callada" [40]). A la impossibilitat normal dels pares d'esborrar les seves frustracions a través de la vida dels fills s'hi afegeix la negativa de Jaumet de compartir amb la mare els detalls de la seva vida adolescent ("no hi ha manera de guaitar, ni per una petita escletxa, dins el món dels seus sentiments" [20]). Irònicament, mare i fill comparteixen un mateix desig de llibertat i de revolta, i Jaumet ho mostra amb la seva militància estudiantil, oposant-se a lleis universitàries i lluitant per ideals de justícia en un context històric, (els primers anys del postfranquisme) que era prou fèrtil per aquesta classe de lluites i d'ideals. I ambdós arriben a una pèrdua absoluta de la llibertat que buscaven, ell amb la mort (a una manifestació estudiantil), ella amb la presó (per haver disparat contra un policia amb la confusió posterior a la mort del fill).

La privació de llibertat que per a la narradora suposa la presó és una extensió real d'una altra mena d'empresonament que prové de l'experiència de la institució de la maternitat i que s'ha anat expressant, a la seva imaginació tenyida de demència, amb un embaràs imaginari, expressió simbòlica de tot el que la lliga a la terra. I en les reaccions davant aquest embaràs són clares les dues actituds contraposades davant la terra: mentre per a ella és el lligam per excel·lència ("estic embarassada, esper un fill que no desig, que em subjuga, que em deixa coixa,...que mentre ell pren cos, a mi m'escapça les ànsies, la idea de llibertat que havia anat concebent" [123-24]), la narradora veu en el marit una voluntat de control i poder consistent amb la mentalitat d'amo de la terra ("Un fill meu, va riure ell, tossint, i tu tornes ésser meva" [110]).

Davant l'embaràs imaginari els altres personatges en constaten la inexistència però són incapaços d'esbrinar-ne les implicacions; per exemple, quan el jove de la consulta del psiquiatra la visita ("A punt de tenir un fill? -ha rigut més, encara-. I a on el duus? Si estàs seca!" [146]). I a la presó:

> jo havia demanat un metge, car jo no em puc quasi moure: les cames inflades, el ventre tibant, els pits estibats de llet, tot jo vessat; però ell, groller, segur, revingut, ulls de rata, m'ha enflocat:
> -Es posi tranquil·la, tot això que té dedins només és vent (152).

Aquest darrera frase, que clou la novel·la, posa de relleu una vegada més la interrelació dels dos centres principals del sistema simbòlic de la novel·la, l'aire i la terra. L'embaràs s'ha associat amb la terra, amb la impossibilitat de dur a terme la seva realització com a dona, empresonada en el paper de mare, connotació que es confirma aquí amb la imatge de l'aire empresonat i sense sortida: el vent, és a dir, les ànsies que té dins ella no ha pogut trobar sortida i s'ha convertit en terra empresonadora. D'aquí que la cambra a la presó sigui, idòniament, "apta per a un cadàver: llarguera, estreta, baixa, en la qual, les ànsies de viure et cauen pel trespol i es fan miques" (152), ja que ella, com a dona, està morta: no ha pogut arribar a néixer, no ha estat possible el part que imaginava en què ella seria infant, mare i comadrona al mateix temps, és a dir, naixeria donant-se vida a ella mateixa.

Veiem, per tant, que el "delicte" de la narradora ha consistit en la denúncia que suposa identificar, mitjançant el simbolisme de la novel·la, el cos femení com a presó en tant que "locus" on s'estableixen les relaciones de poder basades en una definició masculina de l'espai femení que aliena la dona del seu propi cos i del seu propi desig:

> Tot va començar quan me'n vaig adonar...que tot lo que guardava davall es vestit era meu i era jo, que tot m'obeïa i no vaig saber què fer-ne (56-7).

I aquesta necessitat de saber què fer-ne del propi cos, de construir de bell nou l'espai femení, és no només l'eix central de *Quilòmetres de tul per a un petit cadàver* sinó també una constant a la narrativa d'Antonia Vicens que, en conjunt, s'erigeix com a profunda reflexió sobre les implicacions socials e ideològiques de l'experiència femenina.

Dept. of Languages and Literatures
University of Guelph
Guelph, Ont., CANADA N1G 2W1

NOTES FINALS

[1] Betty Friedan, *The Feminine Mystique* 1963 (New York: Bantam, 1984). Encara que el llibre de Friedan es concentra especialment en el context nord-americà dels anys cinquanta, és una important contribució als estudis feministes perquè il·lumina un dels aspectes més constants de la ideologia patriarcal al llarg de la història. Friedan

formula amb gran lucidesa la devastació provocada per una ideologia que entén la realització femenina només en termes de la seva dedicació a la llar, devastació tant a nivell de la dona i el seu sentit d'identitat com a nivell de la societat que perd l'energia creadora i productiva d'una part dels seus membres.

[2] Adrienne Rich, *Of Woman Born: Motherhood as Experience and Institution* (1976; New York and London: Norton, 1986): 13.

[3] Antònia Vicens, *Quilòmetres de tul per a un petit cadàver* (Barcelona: Laia, 1982): 126.

[4] Luce Irigaray, *Le Corps-à-corps avec la mère* (Montréal: Editions de la pleine lune, 1981): 15.

[5] Gaston Bachelard, *La Terre et les rêveries du repos* (Paris: José Corti, 1948).

[6] Bachelard, *Idem,* p. 122.

[7] Rich 13.

[8] Gaston Bachelard, *Air and Dreams: An Essay on the Imagination of Movement,* trans. Edith R. Farrell and C. Frederick Farrell (Dallas: Dallas Institute, 1988).

[9] El tractament de la follia a la narrativa d'Antònia Vicens coincideix amb les consideracions teòriques d'aquells psicòlegs, sociòlegs i crítics literaris d'orientació feminista que tendeixen a la consideració d'elements culturals i socials com a causes determinants dels problemes mentals de les dones. Per una visió de la relació entre dona, follia i literatura, veure: Sandra Gilbert i Susan Gubar, *The Madwoman in the Attic: The Woman Writer and the Nineteenth-Century Literary Imagination* (New Haven, Yale U. P., 1979); Marilyn Yalom, *Maternity Mortality and the Literature of Madnes* (University Park and London: Penn. St. U.P., 1985); Barbara Hill Rigney, *Madness and Sexual Politics in the Feminist Novel* (Madison: Wisconsin U.P., 1978); Phyllis Chesler, *Women and Madness* (New York: Doubleday, 1972).

Edward J. Neugaard

INITIAL AND CLOSING SET PHRASEOLOGY IN CATALAN FOLKTALES

Modern Catalan folktales of the *Märchen* or fairy-tale variety bear the name *rondalles*, which is similar in meaning to the English term "rounds."[1] These tales have existed in oral tradition in the Catalan-speaking lands throughout the centuries, but it was only a mere hundred years ago that they were first collected and published. About thirty-five such *rondalla* collections exist, the largest of which, the *Aplec de rondaies mallorquines* of Antoni Alcover, contains some 322 tales published in 24 volumes.[2]

Opening and closing formulas do not appear in all these printed collections. There are several possible reasons for this. One is that the folklorist who collected the stories from his informants sometimes may have felt they were childish and/or obscene, which, admittedly, they were in many instances. Another possibility is that the collector or editor felt they were superfluous and served no important purpose and, therefore, could be omitted in their published form. All compilers of these tales affirm, however, that their informants more often than not included either an initial or a closing set phraseology, or both, in the telling of their tale. Similar formulas are to be found universally in European fairy tales. All English-speaking children are familiar with the opening phrase "Once upon a time..."

The purpose of these beginning and ending phrases have been the subject of considerable conjecture on part of folklorists. Joan Amades, one of a small number of Catalan folklorists, was the opinion that these formulas were the remnants of ancient religious rituals. According to Amades all prayers, psalms and other religious utterances originally had an opening and closing formula. He speculates that in more recent times these formulaic set phrases were used to bring good luck or to ward off evil spirits.[3]

The French folklore scholar Paul Sébillot has compared these formula to the sign of the cross made before and after the Rosary and certain other Christian prayers. He further points out that Moslems begin all prayers with the set phrase "In the name of Allah, who is forgiving and merciful."[4]

William Bascom, in his folktale typology study, says of these formulas: "In some societies the conventional opening formula which introduces a folktale gives warning to the listener that the narrative which follows is fiction, and that it does not call for belief; and this notice may be repeated in the closing formula. These nominees serve as a frame to enclose folktales, and to set them apart from myths and legends, from normal conversation, and from other forms of serious discourse."[5]

Rosa-Alicia Ramos, in her study of opening and closing formulas in Galician folktales, found that not all her informants used these set phrases and believes that they were "contingent on the structure and the function of the narration rather than on the fancy or the style of the narrator."[6] She also points out that many of the beginning phrases in the tales she collected were not repetitive formulas as such, but rather initial situations, which introduce the listener (or reader) to the characters that are about to appear: "...the opening displays the fictional aspect of the ensuing tale, it almost always includes a reference to the main character(s) too."[7]

This same term, "initial situation" is the same one used by Vladimir Propp in his *Morphology of the Folktale* to refer to the opening presentation of the *dramatis personae* in the folktale. Although Propp asserts that this initial situation is not a *function*, he believes it to be an important *morphological element* of the folktale.[8]

In her book *El cuento folklórico: una aproximación a su estudio* Rosa-Alicia Ramos further states that "in contrast to myths and legends, fictional stories, fairy tales and farcical tales usually begin with an introductory formula which alludes to the non-temporality and vagueness of place...to the observations of Bascom, we wish to add that the fairy tale differs from other oral narrations in that it also concludes with a formula, which corresponds in this case to a structural need and not to a functional explanation as in the case of the initial formula. Since the fairytale is based on a central character, the listener can expect that the protagonist encounter obstacles indefinitely. Through the closing formula...the narrator stresses that the ups and downs of the hero have arrived at their final conclusion and that the frame of the tale that was begun in the introductory formula is now complete."[9]

Generally speaking, the opening and closing formulas observed in the Catalan folktale collections studied have no particular relationship to the story itself, aside from introducing the *dramatis personae*, and are often interchangeable. The only exception to this generalization are the closing formulas of tales that end in a wedding, usually when a lowly hero/heroine marries the prince/princess or king. In these closings reference is frequently made to a wedding feast that is to follow. With his reference to a sumptuous banquet the storyteller is most likely attempting to get an invitation to some sort of meal after the narration of his stories.

In many printed collections of Catalan *rondalles* there are more closing formulas than initial ones. This is perhaps due to the assumption on the part of editors that opening formulas were even more naive, simplistic and unnecessary than the closing ones.

The opening statement of the storyteller usually sets the scene and presents the *dramatis personae*: "There was a king who had only one daughter..." "There was a mother with three sons..." They frequently are set to verse, as can been seen by the following example in the Catalan original:

> Això era i no era
> i bon viatge faci la cadernera,
> per vosaltres un picoti
> i per mi una quartera
> del bon blat que es bat a l'era,
> i el bé que se'n vagi,
> i qui bé faci que bé trobi
> i el dolent que mal hagi.

Many others, however, do not rime:

> Vet aquí que en aquell temps
> dels set moliners,
> que tres eren lladres
> i quatre usurers.

Some initial formulas seem to be intended to ward off evil spirits with a type of magical incantation. Here is an example of this type:

> That was and it was not,
> may the evil go away,
> and the good come.
> He who is good,
> may he have good luck,
> and he who is evil,
> may he suffer the fires of hell.

Many opening statements attempt to situate the story about to be told in some remote, enchanted time when animals, trees and rocks could speak:

> Behold that in that time
> beasts spoke,
> and persons remained silent.
> And behold in that time
> beasts spoke,
> trees sang,
> and rocks walked.

Another rather strange reference, of which there are several examples, is to the "thirteen or fourteen winds." In modern Catalan folklore only eight are commonly designated. This was apparently done to give the story a more archaic, other-worldly flavor:

> Behold in that time
> there were fourteen winds,
> of which seven were good,
> and seven evil.

Others attempt to transport the listener back to a magical time of easy wealth:

> Behold in those times
> straw was made into compost,
> and from the compost came silver.

Social satire plays a significant role in many opening phrases, with certain groups singled out for ridicule, such as millers and students:

> Behold in those times
> of every seven students,
> three were asses and four were brigands.
> Behold in those times
> of seven millers,
> three were thieves
> and four usurers.

Several opening formulas tell of a distant time when criminals had their noses cut off as punishment. Thus a time when everyone had a nose was thought of as an idyllic, crime-free time. To the modern reader this reference has undoubtedly lost its original meaning:

> Behold that
> in a certain corner of the world,
> where everybody had a nose.
> Behold that
> in a town where
> everybody had a nose...

Perhaps the most common motif in the opening statements is a reference to the veracity, or lack thereof, of the story about to be told:

> The story comes,
> the story goes,
> if it is not a lie
> then it is true.
> If it is not a lie
> a sack of flour,
> if it is true,
> a sack of wheat.
> The story goes
> I tell you a pile of stories and foolish things,
> some will be lies and the others will be true.

Another recurring theme in the opening set phraseology are admonitions to the listener to pay attention to the story to be told and to profit from it:

> You should know and understand
> and understand and know
> that once upon a time...
> I'll tell you a story
> as well as I know how.
> If you listen to it
> you will hear it;

> he who doesn't hear it
> will not know it.

Closing formulas are much more common in both the original oral tales and in their printed versions in the Catalan folktales examined. As mentioned earlier, most folklorists agree that they are nearly always present in the original relating of the tale by the informant.

Prof. Ramos speculates that the closing formula "aids in identifying a tale's conclusion...and reminds the listener that what has been heard is purely imaginary; it also indicates that no new developments will follow.[10]

The most common type of closing statement that we find in the Catalan folktale is a combination of nonsense words with a line or two in verse to indicate that the story is over. As the nonsense words are most often onomatopoeic in nature they cannot be translated and, as the rhyme they produce is essential, I will leave them in their original Catalan form:

> Catacric-catacrac
> the story is over
> The story is told
> turururat.
> A la cric-cric
> the tale is already told;
> a la cric-crac
> the story is finished.

Some folklorists, including Joan Amades, believe that this type of formula, with its onomatopoeic rhyme, had its origins in ancient magical incantations.[11]

In many closing statement cats are mentioned:

> And, tururat,
> the story is ended
> with the excrement of a cat.

> Cric-crac,
> the story is ended.
> Look, look, look
> up there a cat is passing by.

Other animals, such as the dog and the rooster are occasionally mentioned:

> You are going to take a long trip
> and on the way you are going to find a chicken;
> on the way you are going to find a dog;
> on the way you are going to find a cat;
> and, behold, the story is ended.
> And they are going to give a great dinner;
> first they are going to eat chicken on a spit
> and then stuffed capon and afterwards a skinned cat;
> and the story is finished.

The fox and the wolf, protagonists of many animal fables, are also mentioned in closing formulas. As in the fables, the fox always manages to out-smart the dullard wolf. Occasionally the story-teller alleges that the fox has grabbed the story itself and has carried it off to his lair.

> And catatric-catatrac
> the story has ended
> and tuuuuut (nonsense word)
> the fox has come
> and has carried it off with him
> to his hole and has remained there.

Another very common motif in the final formulas of the Catalan *rondalla* is the mention of an afterlife. The story-teller expresses the wish that he and his audience be reunited in Heaven with the protagonists of the story just told.

> And up there in Heaven
> they and us will all be together.
> And they were happy
> and as they were happy we too can be
> and we will see them together in Heaven.

Almost always these formulas end with an "Amen," as if a prayer were being said.

A linguistical curiosity in several of these religious closing statements is the use of the Catalan word *fust*, literally meaning "wood." Ever since the fourteenth century Catalan woodcarvers have used this word, which refers to the wood of the Holy Cross and, by extension, to Our Saviour.

> And behind the door ("on the back of the door")
> there is a *fust* (here probably a crucifix)
> and it is ended. Amen, Jesus.
> And at the gates of Heaven
> they say that there is a *fust*
> and it has ended. Amen, Jesus.

Some closing verses seem to have the purpose of placing a curse on the listener who refuses to believe the story just told.

> And he who doesn't want to believe it
> will not drink wine from the gourd
> nor will he go out to dance in the plaza.

At times the storyteller uses an ending statement to convince the listener that the events narrated in the story have just happened and that he has rushed to the scene in order to relate them to the audience present.

> And they stayed there
> and I came here
> in order to tell it to you.

> And we went together as far as... (some town is named)
> and there we left each other
> and I came here in order to be able to tell you
> that which I had just heard.

As many *rondalles* end with a wedding feast, the *rondallaires* often say that they were not given anything to eat at these feasts that they supposedly attended, or that the food they were given was eaten up on the way to the story-telling session by some animal. The reason for this assertion is obvious—so they will be given food and drink by the audience. Here are a few examples:

> And they were there and I here,
> and they didn't give me anything for the road.
> And I came with a big hunk of cheese,
> and the cats on the way, meow, meow,
> didn't leave me not even a little bite.
> And they gave me a plate of hazelnuts,
> which I lost on the way.

A rather bizarre twist occurs at the end of several tales when the storyteller invites his listeners to eat the story that he has just told them.

> And that is the *rondalla* of...
> if you like it, eat if fried
> or eat it roasted;
> and if you don't like it,
> throw it on the table.

Many folktales examined have ending statements that make no sense today. Perhaps there is a reference to some long-forgotten folk belief or legend. One such enigmatic statement is as follows:

> On top of the mountain there is a shoemaker
> who makes his shoes out of paper,
> and he makes a few out of pork fat,
> and the cat goes there and takes a spoonful.

Another rather unusual ending involves the storyteller striking persons in the audience:

> They are going to give me a jug of wine,
> and for you a sack of blows,
> which I am now going to give you.
> The story has ended with a quince,
> and the story has ended with a good blow.

In addition to striking his audience, the storyteller often insults his listeners, like a modern-day stand-up comic. To the newlyweds present he may tell them that they will have three children, always of the same sex. He tells them what the first two will become and then pauses. The couple then naively ask him what the third will be and he insults them with some scatological reference:

> And you are going to have three daughters;
> the oldest one is going to give you a big loaf of bread;
> the middle one a little loaf of bread
> and the little one a *coca.* (a type of Catalan pastry)
> The oldest one with that large loaf of bread
> is going to find a king for a husband;
> the middle one with her little loaf of bread
> is going to find a prince.

He then pauses until one of them asks about the third daughter. He then strikes out with this insulting reply:

> A good piece of shit for your mouth!

Here is another example:

> And you are going to have three daughters,
> one is going to be named Maria,
> another Joanne and the third Agnes.
> Maria is going to marry a king, Joanne a prince.
> ... And Agnes? [One of the couple asks]

Kiss my ass, for I don't know anything more about it!

As can be expected, these insulting formulas rarely appear in the printed versions, especially those published as children's literature, which is often the case with Catalan *rondalla* collections.

Perhaps the most common and typical closing formula is the one in which the storyteller speculates as to whether the protagonists of the story are still alive or, if dead, if they are in Heaven or Hell.

> And if they are not dead they are alive,
> and if they are not alive they are dead.
> And they must still be alive if they are not dead,
> and we can see each other if it is convenient
> and if a bolt of lightning has not killed them,
> they are still there.
> And he went off to Hell,
> where, if he is not cold,
> he will be hot.

The veracity of the story just told is also a very common motif of the closing formulas. The *rondallaire* tries to convince his gullible audience that the fairytale really did occur exactly as narrated.

> And all of this is as true
> as if it had never happened.
> And the story is ended;
> he who believes it will fly to Heaven,
> and he who doesn't will go to roast in Hell.

Sometimes, however, the *contaire* does just the opposite and makes fun of the credulous listener who might actually believe his story.

> And the story is ended
> and he who has listened to it
> has been a good lad,
> and he who has believed it
> is a real fool.

In still another variant, the storyteller tells the person who doesn't believe the story to go and check on its veracity himself.

> And he who doesn't want to believe it,
> let him go and see it.
> And he who doesn't believe it,
> let him go to look for himself.

Sometimes the storyteller tells the listener that, if he didn't like the story, he should tell a better one himself.

> And he who knows more about it,
> let him tell more about it.
> And he who didn't like the story that I have told,
> let him tell a better one.

In conclusion, the beginning and ending formulas in the Catalan folktale have not been sufficiently studied and represent a treasure trove of linguistic, sociological and folkloristic information. The initial set phrases are used to set the mood of the story to be told, to make it seem as if it took place in a non-real time and place and to introduce the characters. The closing formulas, on the other hand, seem to have a much wider variety of uses: to inform the reader that the story just told is or is not true, to tell the audience that they will meet the protagonists of the story in the after-life, to beg for food after the telling of the tale and many other purposes, some of which appear to be unique to the Catalan folktale.

Modern Languages and Linguistics
University of South Florida
Tampa, FL 33620

ENDNOTES

[1] In Stith Thompson's *Motif-Index of Folk-Literature*, 6 vols. (Bloomington: Indiana U. P., 1955-1957) the term "rounds" is used for a type of tale which begins over and over again. It is motif Z17.

[2] Antoni Alcover, *Aplec de rondaies mallorquines* (Palma de Mallorca: Moll, 1982-1983).

[3] Joan Amades, *Folklore de Catalunya: La rondallística* (Barcelona: Selecta, 1982): 131.

[4] Paul Sébillot, *Le Folk-lore* (Paris, 1913): 43.

[5] William Bascom, "The Forms of Folklore: Prose Narratives," *Journal of American Folklore* 78 (1965): 6.

[6] Rosa-Alicia Ramos, "Opening and Closing Formulas and Patterns in Galician Oral Narrative," *Southern Folklore* 46 (1989): 53.

[7] Ramos, "Opening and Closing Formulas," 55.

[8] Vladirmir Propp, *Morphology of the Folktale* (Austin: U. Texas P., 1968): 25.

[9] Rosa-Alicia Ramos, *El cuento folklórico: una aproximación a su estudio* (Madrid: Pliegos, 1988): 22-23. [This quotation was translated from the Spanish by the author of this article.]

[10] Ramos, "Opening and Closing Formulas," 56.

[11] Amades, *Folklore de Catalunya: La rondallística* 127.

Edward J. Neugaard

PER A UNA BIBLIOGRAFIA DE LA RONDALLA

Aquesta bibliografia de la rondalla representa les col·leccions rondallístiques que l'autor ha pogut recollir com a part de les seves investigacions sobre el tema. Hi ha poques obres escrites sobre el gènere—de critica literària gairebé res. Moltes d'aquestes col·leccions de rondalles són difícils de trobar i no totes figuren en les grans biblioteques (la Biblioteca de Catalunya i la Biblioteca Nacional a Madrid). Com es pot veure, en els últims anys varies col·leccions de rondalles s'han editat novament. A vegades és difícil d'establir la relació entre algunes col·leccions. Els comentaris sobre l'edició en qüestió apareixen entre claudàtors.

1. Col·leccions de rondalles

Adlert Noguerol, Miquel. *Recull de contes valencianes.* Barcelona: Albertí, 1958.

Alcántara Pena, Pedro de. *Cuentos mallorquines,* 1884.

Alcover i Sureda, Antoni M. [Es Jordi des Racó]. *Aplec de rondaies mallorquines d'en Jordi des Racó.* 24 vols. Palma de Mallorca: Moll, 1982-1983.

---. *Les millors rondalles de Mallorca.* Ciutat de Mallorca, 1946; Palma de Mallorca: Moll, 1985.

---. Andreu Ferrer Ginard i Joan Castelló Guasch. *Rondaies de les Illes Balears*. Palma: Moll, 1975.

---. *Rondalles mallorquines*. Palma de Mallorca: Moll, 1960.

---. *Folk Tales of Mallorca: A Selection from "L'Aplec de rondaies mallorquines" de Mossèn Antoni M. Alcover*. Trad., David Huelin. [Traduccions a l'anglès]. Palma de Mallorca: Moll, 1988.

Amades, Joan. *Les cent millors rondalles populars*. Barcelona, 1953.

---. *Folklore de Catalunya: Rondallística*. Barcelona: Selecta, 1950. [Amb 662 rondalles és la col·lecció de rondalles més extensiva].

---. *Les millors rondalles populars catalanes*. 4a ed. Barcelona: Selecta, 1981.

---. *Noves rondalles populars*. Barcelona: Selecta, 1985.

---. *Tradicions i llegendes*. Barcelona, 1947.

Arxiduc Lluis Salvador. *Rondayes de Mallorca*. Wirzburg [Würzburg]: Woerl, 1895; Arxiu de Tradicions Populars, 16. Palma de Mallorca: de Olañeta 1982.

---. *Obres completes*. Barcelona: Selecta, 1951.

Badenes i Dalmau, Francesc. *Rondalles del poble*. Barcelona, 1900.

Balaguer, Victor. *Historias y leyendas*. Barcelona, 1899.

Bergà i Boix, Josep. *Llegendes de la comarca d'Olot*. Olot, 1914.

Bertran i Bros, Pau. *El rondallari català*. Barcelona: Giró, 1909; Estudi preliminar i edició de Josep M. Pujol. Arxius del Folklore Català, 2. Barcelona: Alta Fulla, 1989.

---. *Rondalles populars catalanes*. Barcelona: Giró, 1908.

---. *Rondalles tradicionales*. Incomplet. [13 rondalles].

---. *Rondalleta*. Barcelona, 1880. [En vers].

---. *Rondallística*. Barcelona, 1888.

---. *Tradicions populars catalanes*. Barcelona, s.a. [Sembla ésser el mateix que l'obra de Caseponce].

Bonet, J. *Recull de contes balears*. Barcelona: Albertí, 1956.

Briz, Francesc Pelai. *La Panolla*. Barcelona: Ed. Catalana, 1922.

Camps Mercadal, Francisco. *Folklore menorquín*. 2 vols. Mahón: Sintés, 1918.

Canigó, Jordi. *Les rondalles de l'avi*. Barcelona: Bonavia, 1929.

Capacete i Novo, Lluís. *Rondalles Populars*. Lleida: Diputació de Lleida, 1985.

Caseponce [Casaponce], Esteve. *Contes vallespirenchs*. Barcelona, s.a.

---. *Rondalles*. 5a ed. Barcelona: Balmes, 1972.

---. *Rondalles del Vallespir*. Barcelona: Foment de Pietat, 1917; El Tinter dels Clàssics, 1. Barcelona: Abadia de Montserrat, 1993.

Castelló Guasch, Juan. *Rondaies i contes d'Eivissa*. Palma Mallorca: Alfa, 1961.

---. *Rondalles d'Eivissa*. Palma: Moll, 1955.

---. *Rondalles de Formentera*. Palma: Alfa, 1976.

---. *Rondaies eivissenques de quan el bon Jesús anava pel món*. Palma: Alfa, 1974.

---. *Rondaies eivissenques i contes de sa majora*. Palma: Alfa, 1976.

Constans, Lluis G. *Rondalles*. Banyoles: Estudis Comarcals, 1981.

---. *Llegendes muntanyenques*. Barcelona: Foment de Pietat, 1925.

Desclot, Miquel. *Rondalla va mentida va*. Barcelona: Onda, 1982.

Farnés, Sebastià. *Narraciones populares catalanas*. Barcelona: Bibl. Universal, 1893. [Traduccions al castellà].

---. *Rondalles*. Barcelona: La Renaxensa, 19??

Ferrer Ginard, Andreu. *Rondalles de Menorca*. 2 vols. 4a ed. Menorca: Nura, 1974-1979.

---. *Folklore Balear. Vol. I. Ciutadella: Vda. Fabregas, 1914; Palma: Cort, 1965.*

---. *Rondalles populars de diferents autors i països*. Palma: Artà, 19??

Galiana, Lluis. *Rondalla de rondalles*. València, 1931. [No és una rondalla de debò].

Gomis Llambies, Juan. *Rondalles: Aplec de les comarques de Catalu nya adaptat per a servir de text a les escoles*. Girona: Gerun dense, 1922.

Gonzàlez i Caturla, Joaquim. *Rondalles de l'alacantí*. Alacant: Inst. Gil-Albert, 1985.

---. *Rondalles del Baix Vinolopó: Contes populars*. Alacant: Inst. Gil Albert, 1987.

Gonzàlez Martí, Manuel. *Contes del pla i de la muntanya, de la València medieval*. València, 1947.

Jané, Albert. *Rondalles de Catalunya*. Barcelona: Casanovas, 1982.

Karlinger, Felix i Johannes Pogl. *Katalanische Märchen*. Diederichs, 1989.

Martí i Gadea, Joaquim. *Encisam de totes herbes.* València: 1891.

Martínez i Martínez, Francesc. *Coses de la meua terra (La Marina).* 2 vols. València, 1912 i 1920. [Tanda I, 1912; tanda II, 1920].

———. *Folklore valencià.* València, 1923.

Masiera, A. *Rondalles de Poble.* Barcelona, 1900.

Maspons i Labrós, Francesc. *Lo rondallaire.* Barcelona: Barcino, 1930.

———. *Contes populars catalans.* Barcelona: Barcino, 1952.

———. *El poll i la puça.* Barcelona: La Galera, 1977.

———. *Lo Rondallaire (Qüentos populars catalans).* Barcelona: A. Verdaguer, 1871.

———. *Tradicions del Vallès.* Barcelona: Barcino-Ariel, 1952.

Mestres, Apel·les. *Tots els contes.* Barcelona: Ales Esteses, s.a.

Mestres i Freixes, J. *Rondalles a la vora del foc.* San Boi de Llobregat: Mall, 1986.

Milà i Fontanals, Manuel. *Gaceta de Barcelona.* 1853. [207 rondalles].

Morey, Pere. *Rondalles pels qui els agrada la historia.* Palma: Moll, 1984.

———. *Rondalles pels qui les saben totes.* Palma: Moll, 1981.

Pascual Tirado, Josep. *Tomba-Tossals.* Castelló: Societat Castellonense, 1930; València: L'Estel, 1988.

Pérez Llopis, A. *La rondalla espanyola.* Castelló, 1984.

Pi Ferrer, Salvadó. *Rondalla.* Barcelona: Pascual, 1975.

La Rondalla: Setmani Català. Barcelona. Any I (1874), Nos. 2-8.

Rondalla del Dijous. Arxiu Tradicions Populars, 21-32. Palma: de Olañeta, 1982.

Rondalles de Catalunya. Albert Jané. Barcelona: Casanovas, 1975.

Rondalles noves. Dir. J. M. Esteve Victòria. 3 vols. Barcelona, 1912.

Rondalles de la Mainada. Barcelona: Artis, s.a.

Rondaies de Mallorca. Barcelona: Casanovas, 1975.

Rondalles valencianes. 3 vols. València: Entitats Culturals al País Valencià, 1984-.

Sabrafin, Gabriel. *Leyendas tradiciones, cuentos fabulosos y otros relatos fantásticos de las islas de Cabrera, Formentera, Eivissa, Menorca y Mallorca.* Palma: de Olañeta, 1982. [En castellà].

Sales, Joan. *Rondalles escollides de Guimerà, Caseponce i Alcover.* Barcelona: Ariel, 1950.

---. *Rondalles escollides de Ramon Llull, Mistral i Verdaguer.* Barcelona: Ariel, 1949.

Scanu, Pasqual. *Rondalles alguereses.* Barcelona: Dalmau, 1985.

Serra i Boldú, Valeri. *Aplec de rondalles.* 2a ed. Barcelona: Abadia de Montserrat, 1981.

---. *Rondalles meravelloses.* 3a ed. Barcelona: Abadia de Montserrat, 1984.

---. *Rondalles populars.* 4 vols. Barcelona: Abadia de Montserrat, 1984-1985.

Valor, Enric. *Obra literària completa.* 2 vols. València: GORG, 1975.

---. *Rondalles valencianes.* València: Torre, 1950-.

---. *Rondalles valencianes.* 10 vols. València: Federació d'Entitats

Culturals del País Valencià, 1985-.

Verdaguer, Jacint. *Rondalles.* Barcelona: Ilustració Catalana, 1905.

Vidal Alcover, Jaume. *Recull de llegendes.* Barcelona: Dopesa, 1978.

---. *Antologia de contes, rondalles i llegendes, exemples i facècies.* Barcelona: Diàfora, 1981.

Vila, Joan [Dibuixant]. *Les rondalles populars catalanes.* Barcelona: la Magrana, 1985. [El mateix que Bergà i Boix, Josep, més abaix].

Wert, Georg A. *Märchentraum der Balearen: 30 Märchen aus Mallorca, Menorca, Ibiza und Formentera.* Bern: Erpf, 1984.

2. Estudis sobre les rondalles

Almodovar, R. Antonio. "Les Contes de tradicion orale en Espagne sur leur variabilité systematique, leur sens." En *La Variabilité dans la litterature orale/From One Tale...to the Other: Variability in Oral Literature* (Eds. Veronika Gorog-Karady i Michele Chiche). Paris: CNRS, 1990.

Ferrer Massanet, Rafael. *Iniciació a las "Rondaies Mallorquines" de Mossèn Alcover.* Felanix, 1963.

Grimalt Gomila, Josep Antoni. "La catalogació de les rondalles de Mossèn Alcover com a introducció a llur estudi." *Randa 7* (1978), 5-30.

---. *La catalogació de les rondalles de Mossèn Alcover com a introducció a llur estudi.* Tesis doctoral. Univ. de Barcelona, 1975.

---. *Classificació de les rondalles de Mossèn Alcover: Introducció a llur estudi/ resum de la tesi presentada per assolir al grau de doctor en filologia per Josep Antoni Grimalt Gomila.* Barcelona: Univ. de Barcelona, 1979. Pp. 16.

Janer, Maria de la Pau. *Les rondalles del cicle de l'espós transformat.* Barcelona: Abadia de Montserrat, 1992.

Llompart, Josep Maria. "Les *Rondaies mallorquines*: Un "best seller." En *Setmana del llibre editat a Mallorca (1a: 1971: Ciutat de Mallorca).* Pp. 5-7. Ciutat de Mallorca: Tous, 1971. Pp. 24.

Lluch, Gemma. *De princesses i herois: La rondallística meravellosa d'Enric Valor.* València: Generalitat, 1988.

Moll, Francesc de B. *Aspectes marginals d'un home de combat: Mossèn Antoni M. Alcover.* Barcelona: Curial, 1983. Pp. 180.

---. "Le Censure moral de Mossèn Alcover a les seves 'Rondalles mallorquines'." En *Homenaje a Elias Serra.* La Laguna: Univ. de La Laguna, 1970. Pp. 12.

Neugaard, Edward J. "The Rondayes de Mallorca of the Archduke Salvator: An Index of Motifs and Tale Types." *Campo Abierto* II, 8 (1991), 1-21.

Oriol, Carme. "Revision of Amades' Classification of the Catalan Folktales." *Fabula* 31: 304-312.

Pellicer Borràs, Joan. *La "Rondalla de Rondalles" de Lluis Galiana: Estudi lingüístic i edició.* València: Univ. de València, 1986.

Violant Ribera, Ramona. *La rondalla i la llegenda: Contribució a l'estudi de la literatura folklòrica catalana.* Barcelona: Alta Fulla, 1990.

Modern Languages and Linguistics
University of South Florida
Tampa, FL 33620

Josep M. Solà-Solé

SOBRE EL "CANT ESPIRITUAL" DE JOAN MARAGALL

Una de les composicions més conegudes i encomiades de la poesia catalana moderna és, sens dubte, el "Cant Espiritual" de Joan Maragall. La seva dimensió humana, les diverses interpretacions que possibilita, en fi, el seu dramatisme que creix per acabar amb una afirmació rotunda, sumat tot a les seves proporcions adequades (45 versos), fan que aquesta composició sigui coneguda, totalment o parcialment, de molta gent.

Nosaltres voldríem emprendre en aquest estudi una doble anàlisi. Per una part, una anàlisi estructural a base de la nova metodologia analítico-quantitativa o computacional. I per això, com és degut, compararem el "Cant Espiritual" amb composicions de tema més o menys semblant ("Cant Espiritual" d'Ausiàs March, "Sum vermis" de Jacint Verdaguer, "Nabí" [fragment] de Josep Carner, "Tots hi serem al Port amb la desconeguda" de J. V. Foix[1]). Per l'altra, portarem a terme una anàlisi conceptual i de fons de la composició maragalliana, procurant aportar nous elements o reforçar alguns que no semblen haver estat degudament assenyalats.

a) Anàlisi estructural.

1. El "Cant Espiritual" de Joan Maragall (a partir d'ara CEMarag) consta de 45 versos decasíl·labs de tipus tradicional, és a dir, el que, per exemple, trobem ja en el "Cant Espiritual" d'Ausiàs March (a partir d'ara CEMarch). El seu accent cau preferentment a la sexta síl·laba, però en el CEMarag hi enregistrem un 15,555% de casos d'accentuació 4-8.[2] Cal dir, tanmateix, que en el CEMarch trobem, en canvi, a part l'accentuació a la sexta (41,105%) i a la 4-8 (25,892%) un bon número de versos d'accentuació anapèstica 4-7 (29,910%).[3]

2. Les vocals accentuades (les d'accent intern i de rima) són en el CEMarag predominantment les de timbre -o- (26,804%), seguides de les de timbre -e- (24,742%), -a- (20,618%), -i- (17,525%) i -u- (10,309%). Tant el percentatge de -o- com, fins a un cert punt, el de -u- no deixa de sorprendre, ja que, dins el conjunt vocàlic de la composició, aquests dos timbres estan representats per sols un 15,523% i un 9,025% respectivament, cosa que podria apuntar a una possible relació amb el tema central del poema.[4]

3. El CEMarag consta d'un total de 381 termes, agrupats en un corpus de 181 termes morfològicament distintius, implicant un alt coeficient (relació entre el vocabulari total i el número de termes diferenciats) de reducció: 2,10. Dit d'una altra manera: el vocabulari diferenciat queda reduït a un 47,506% del total, percentatge més baix que en els altres tres textos contemporanis (en el de Verdaguer, reducció a un 53,975%; en el de Carner a un 50,659%; en el de Foix a un 53,515%), però per damunt del d'Ausiàs March, reduït a un 33,405%. Això assenyalaria, doncs, tant en aquest darrer text com en el de Maragall, una considerable

repetició lèxica.

4. En quant a la llargada de les paraules, cal apuntar que és el CEMarag el que té un terme mig de paraules més curtes: 3,59 lletres per paraula. El segueix de prop el CEMarch amb 3,62 i, ja amb més diferència, Verdaguer amb 3,83 i Carner amb 3,93. En canvi, Foix enregistra un 4,10, és a dir, una ben marcada tendència a l'ús de paraules estructuralment més llargues. Enfront de tots els altres textos, amb paraules tots ells de fins a 12 lletres, el CEMarag sols enregistraria mots amb un màxim de 10.

5. El CEMarag consta d'un total de 23 frases,[5] amb una certa tendència a l'ús de frases relativament curtes, situant-se la majoria d'elles entre els 6 i 10 mots, amb la més llarga de 37. En aquest aspecte, està per sota de tots els altres textos: March 7-18 i màxima de 53; Carner 8-16 i màxima de 44; Verdaguer 9-21 i màxima de 36; Foix 18-19 i màxima de 61.

6. Ara bé, no deixa de sorprendre que d'aquestes 23 frases el 39,130% siguin interrogatives, el 17,391% admiratives o exclamatives i que el 13,043% d'elles acabin amb punts suspensius. La tensió dramàtica que això implicaria (amb dubtes, indecisions i, fins i tot, afirmacions categòriques) quedaria encara més palesa si comparem el nostre text amb els que ens serveixen de base: en el CEMarch un 6,086% de frases interrogatives i un 8,695% de frases admiratives o exclamatives; en el poema de Carner un 3,700% de frases interrogatives i el mateix percentatge d'admiratives; en el text de Foix no hi documentem cap frase interrogativa, però sí un 16,666% d'admiratives i un 4,166% (en realitat sols una) d'acabades amb punts suspensius. Establint encara un major contrast, el "Sum vermis" de Verdaguer no ostenta cap d'aquest

recursos.

7. Deixant de banda 'ésser' i 'haver,' els verbs més freqüents en el CEMarag són 'fer' i 'veure' (1,0495% i 0,787% respectivament del vocabulari total). Hi hauria, doncs, en aquesta obra una certa preferència per l'acció i l'activitat visual. Malgrat que també trobem una preferència similar (juntament amb 'dir' i 'passar') en la composició de Foix, el programa d'ordinador que analitza les distàncies respectives a través de les inter-relacions de freqüències,[6] aproxima molt més, en quant als verbs en general, la composició maragalliana al CEMarch, i això malgrat que aquest darrer insisteix més aviat en 'fer,' 'voler' i 'sentir.'

8. Hi ha en el CEMarag un total de 48 formes verbals personals, les quals, considerant el número de frases (23), dóna una freqüència de 2,08 verbs per frase, proporció que està un xic per sota de la de Foix i del CEMarch i lleugerament per damunt del que observem en l'obra de Carner i de Verdaguer. Ara bé, les 48 formes verbals personals del CEMarag es divideixen en 25 de 3a. persona (52,083%), una de 2a. (2,083%), 11 de 1a. (22,916) i, finalment, també 11 de persona 'vós' (22,916%). Sols Verdaguer presentaria un esquema semblant, però les freqüències són: 24,074% de 1a. persona, 7,407% de 2a., 35,185% de 3a. i, en quant a la forma 'vós,' un força elevat 33,333%. Tant el CEMarag com la composició de Verdaguer evidenciarien, doncs, un diàleg entre un 'jo' i un 'vós,' aquest darrer representat pel 'Senyor,' al qual s'adreçaria el 'jo' en la forma tradicional de cortesia. El CEMarch, en canvi, per dirigir-se a Déu, opta per l'ús del 'tu' de 2a. persona, que remunta a un 16,265%, enfront, però, d'un 35,240% en quant a la de 1a. persona i un 48,493% en quant a la de 3a.

9. No deixa d'ésser interessant remarcar, tanmateix, que mentre el CEMarag estructuralment es presenta com un diàleg entre el 'jo' i el 'vós,' l'èmfasi, marcat per la presència o absència dels pronoms subjecte corresponents, és menys acusat. En efecte, mentre en el CEMarag sols trobem dues formes pronominals de 'jo' (0,524% del vocabulari total) i cap de 'vós,' en el text de Verdaguer enregistrem 4 pronoms subjecte de 1a. persona (0,966%) i 3 de 2a. (0,723%). En canvi, en el CEMarch observem 34 'jo' (1,846%) i 40 'tu' (2,172%). L'èmfasi, doncs, en el 'jo' i en el 'tu/vós,' per més que ja patent en Verdaguer, resulta ésser encara més acusat en el CEMarch, veritable diàleg entre el 'jo' i el 'tu' (Déu).

10. Aquesta mateixa particularitat és notòria si analitzem els pronoms complement ('me,' 'te' i etc.) i els adjectius possessius ('meu,' 'ma' i etc.). Aquests dos elements constitueixen en el CEMarag un total de 5,772% del vocabulari global, amb un 81,818% d'aquest percentatge, és a dir, una quantitat prou predominant, referits a la 1a. persona. En el CEMarch el percentatge d'aquests pronoms és d'un més elevat 8,307%, amb un 72,549% d'ells referits a la 1a. persona. Finalment, en el "Sum vermis" de Verdaguer, seguint l'èmfasi que l'autor posa en l'expressió pronominal, el percentatge és d'un 10,867%, amb un 77,777% d'ells relacionats amb la 1a. persona.

11. Entre els subjectes de les formes verbals de 3a. persona, anotem en el CEMarag certa preferència per 'món' (24,000%) i 'vida' (8,000%). Hi hauria, per tant, en aquesta composició una forta presència d'aquest dos elements. En el "Sum vermis" de Verdaguer, en canvi, marcant un altre to, els subjectes més importants, són 'cós' (7,407%) i 'no-res' (5,555%). Finalment, en el CEMarch hi predominaria com a subjecte,

a part de certa abundància de subjectes indefinits o impersonals, els termes 'fi' i 'fins,' (7,317%), seguits d''esperit' i 'voler' com a substantiu (3,048% cada un).

12. La preocupació de Maragall per l'existència podria veure's en la freqüència de les diferents formes de 'ser/ésser,' que són més abundants en el CEMarag (3,673% del vocabulari total[7]), que en totes les altres composicions. Fins i tot, és quelcom més abundant que en el "Sum vermis" de Verdaguer (3,622%) i, àdhuc, que en el CEMarch (3,352%). Molt més baixa seria la freqüència en Carner (1,057%) i, sobretot, en Foix (1,057%).

13. Donada la preferència per l'acció visual, no és d'estranyar que en el CEMarag un dels substantius més freqüents sigui 'ull/s' (1,312% del vocabulari total), en segon lloc després de 'Senyor' (1,574%). Aquest darrer terme, preferit al de 'Déu,' que no apareix en el CEMarag, posat en condició de vocatiu i en posició generalment accentuada, ajudaria a fer ressaltar una relació de dependència. Aquí encara, i malgrat certes coincidències amb Foix (preeminència de l'òrgan visual), el programa d'ordinador ja al·ludit (#7 i nota 5) aproximaria també més el CEMarag al CEMarch.

14. En el CEMarag l'oposició entre 'Déu/Senyor' i 'home' és molt més favorable al primer (8 a 1). Per altra banda, l'oposició 'vida' i 'mort' és favorable a aquesta darrera (2 a 1), mentre que és inexistent la de 'dia' i 'nit,' car aquest darrer terme no està present en el vocabulari del cant maragallià. Per altra banda, la insistència de Maragall en el terme 'mort' (1,049% del vocabulari total) seria una nota distintiva del CEMarag, ja que, comparativament, sols el CEMarch s'hi acostaria un xic (0,434%).

15. Una notable característica del CEMarag és la notable insistència per part de l'autor en marcar l'espai. Són, en efecte, freqüents els demostratius ('aquell,' 'aquella,' 'aquells,' 'aquelles,' etc.), arribant a un 2,099% del vocabulari total (en CEMarch, el text més pròxim sols assoleix un 1,140%). En quan als adverbis de lloc ('aquí,' 'ací,' 'allà,' 'allí,' 'hi'), aconsegueixen en el CEMarag un 1,836%, percentatge notablement més elevat que, per exemple, en el "Sum vermis" de Verdaguer (0,528%) i, fins i tot, que en el CEMarch (0,651%). Aquest afany de precisió contrastaria, tanmateix, amb la vaguetat donada per un dels versos més significatius del poema: "però on sou, qui ho sap."

16. El to general de la composició maragalliana, marcat pel contrast entre els termes d'expressió o contingut positiu i els de contingut negatiu ('dia'/'nit,' 'vida'/'mort,' 'amor'/'dolor' i etc), resulta ser en el CEMarag clarament positiu, ja que hi predominen en un 3,88 a 1 els termes d'aquesta índole, mostrant el coeficient positiu més elevat de les cinc composicions que contrastem. En general, però, en totes elles predominen els termes positius (1,810 en el CEMarch; 1,480 en Carner i 1,186 en Foix). Una excepció molt inequívoca la trobaríem en el "Sum vermis" de Verdaguer on l'expressió negativa sobrepassa a la positiva en un 1,40 a 1.

17. Malgrat que el CEMarag és reduït en quant al número de frases i a la seva llargària (#5), és, tanmateix, una composició que conté relativament un bon número de conjuncions il·latives ('i'/'ni'/'que') (6,035%), percentatge superat sols per Carner (6,213%). Cal dir, però, que la il·lativa 'i' serveix, sobretot, per a unir dos o tres termes i no pas dues frases (14 de 19 casos, és a dir, una proporció de 1 a 1,37), proporció semblant, per altra banda, a la de Verdaguer, però superior, per

exemple, a la de Carner (1 a 2,428).

18. També el grafema 'que' és prou corrent en el CEMarag (3,410%), amb un percentatge superior a tres de les altres composicions (Verdaguer 1,449%; Foix 1,764%; Carner 1,982%), però lleugerament per sota del CEMarch (3,692%). Aquí encara (i això estaria relacionat amb la manca de subordinació) el 'que' predominant és el 'que' relatiu (2,361%) i no pas el conjuntiu (1,049%). En relació, però, amb aquest fet, observem com en el CEMarch predomina excepcionalment el 'que' conjuntiu (2,715% vers 0,977%).

19. Considerant la totalitat de conjuncions, el CEMarag és la composició que mostra un percentatge més elevat d'elles: 8,921%. I això en front d'un 8,688% en el CEMarch, d'un 6,610% en Carner, d'un 6,272% en Foix i d'un baix 4,347% en Verdaguer. Mentre, però, en el CEMarch anotem una certa varietat de formes ('i,''ni,''que,''doncs,''mes,''o,' 'puig,''perquè,''si'), en el CEMarag observem la manca de 'car' i 'puig' i una relativa abundància de 'si' (6 casos), que marcarien una sèrie de qüestions hipotètiques.

20. Contràriament a l'abundància de conjuncions, en el CEMarag hi anotem una remarcable escassetat de preposicions, que sols arriben a un relativament baix 8,134% (Ausiàs 9,774%; Verdaguer 14,973%; Carner 13,087% i Foix 12,936%, amb en aquest darrer una marcada preferència per 'amb'). Aquesta escassetat és més patent encara si establim la correlació "conjunció" / "preposició" en els cinc textos analitzats. En efecte, en el CEMarag la proporció s'estableix en un 0,91, és a dir, per cada conjunció hi hauria un 0,91 de preposicions. En canvi, en el CEMarch, text que en aquest cas s'aproxima més al CEMarag, la relació

és de 1,12, essent de 1,98 en Carner, en 2,06 en Foix i d'un elevat 3,44 en el "Sum vermis" de Verdaguer.

21. L'aplicació als cinc textos considerats del ja esmentat programa especialment preparat per a assenyalar les inter-distàncies entre tota una sèrie de factors (#5), ens procura el curiós i interessant resultat de que dels tretze factors analitzats (llargura de la frase, llargada de les paraules, lletres o signes presents, mots usats una i més vegades, mots usats una vegada un, dos vegades dos i etc., article i numerals, noms, adjectius, demostratius, verbs, adverbis, pronoms, preposicions i conjuncions), dels cinc textos, els dos que més s'aproximen són el CEMarag i el CEMarch (set casos del tretze). En quant als adverbis, en canvi, el CEMarag s'acostaria més al "Sum vermis" de Verdaguer. Així mateix, en quant als adjectius, el poema maragallià s'aproximaria més a la composició de Foix i, en quant a les preposicions i als pronoms estaria més a prop del "Nabí" de Carner. De tota manera, en aquests tres darrers casos, el segon text més pròxim fóra encara el CEMarch. Finalment, en un factor, la llargura de la frase, el CEMarag s'apartaria considerablement de tots els altres textos. En resum, quedaria ben clar fins a quin punt hi ha una estreta relació estructural, que molt difícilment pot explicar-se exclusivament per l'afinitat temàtica, entre el CEMarag i el CEMarch.

b) Anàlisi intern

1. El CEMarag és, com ja hem assenyalat (#16) una composició predominantment optimista en la qual el poeta dialoga amb el 'Senyor' i li demana per què no podria ser eterna 'aquesta' vida, és a dir, la vida plena d'impactes i gaudiments visuals que Maragall coneixia. Per més

que no hem de perdre de vista que la composició està orientada vers el conflicte humà de la mort, aquesta està emmascarada per la necessitat de (sobre)vivència dels elements sensuals d'aquesta vida.

2. Aquest to optimista ens mena a la nota hedonística que el poema respira, nota ja observada per alguns crítics i que, en el fons del fons, seria predominant i això independentment de si l'autor volia insistir-hi o no. A la fi i al cap, tota obra artística viu una vida independent i té dret a qualsevol recepció per part del lector. Ara bé, aquesta extensió hedonística de gaudiment dels sentits i, sobretot, del sentit de la vista se'ns dóna com una conseqüència de l'home burgès i, més encara, de l'home burgès mediterrani. Es tracta de l'actitud de l'home que, gaudint d'una bona posició social i econòmica (com era la de Maragall), es pot complaure en l'admiració d'un paisatge ple de sol, de mar, de muntanyes i de tot allò que entra pels ulls (un dels termes més freqüents, com hem vist, del CEMarag) i que, tanmateix, no pot ni vol comprendre que hi pugui haver quelcom de més gloriós: "si per mi com aquest no n'hi haurà cap!"

3. Àdhuc la pau cristiana (i no hi ha dubte que Maragall intentava viure-la), no impedeix estimar aquest món tan formós. L'home que creu en Déu i contempla aquest paisatge jo ho té tot i no voldria pas res més: "I no voldré més cel que aquest cel blau." Per això no és massa adequat relacionar la filosofia del CEMarag amb la dels místics cristians, per bé que aquests també sabien admirar i apreciar el paisatge. Però el paisatge dels místics, el "locus amoeneus" de tanta tradició literària, és un paisatge que afavoreix el recolliment i, a través d'aquest, la definitiva trobada amb Déu. En canvi, la contemplació del paisatge, essencialment mediterrani, per part de Maragall, l'apartarien de Déu, d'on la temença

de la mort: "...i temo tant la mort!"

4. Que, dins de tot, estem davant de l'actitud de l'home mediterrani, ho podem percebre encara més clarament si comparem l'essència del CEMarag amb una obra que el poeta sembla tenir present en el moment d'escriure el seu poema i que sempre fou a més una de les fonts més importants de l'obra entera del nostre poeta. Ens referim al Faust de Goethe. Fins i tot en el moment d'escriure el "Cant Espiritual" (moment de probable crisi espiritual), Maragall no podia deixar de pensar en l'obra cabdal del gran escriptor alemany. Això queda ben clar, sobretot, en els versos maragallians: "Aquell que a cap moment li digué "Atura't," / sinó al mateix que li dugué la mort, / jo no l'entenc, Senyor; jo que voldria / aturar tants moments de cada dia / per fe'ls eterns a dintre del meu cor!..." Doncs bé, Faust, l'home enamoradís, però feble, mai no va saber gaudir de la vida, i fou en arribar a l'hora de la mort que va demanar: "Zum Augenblicke dürf ich sagen: / Verweile doch, du bist so schön!" ("Al moment jo diria:/ espera, doncs, ets tan bonic!"[8]) (vv. 11581-82). I encara, més endavant, "Im Vorgefühl von solchem hohen Glück / Geniess ich jetz den höchesten Augenblick" ("En el presentiment d'una felicitat tan gran / gaudeixo ara del moment més elevat"[9]) (vv. 11585-86). A la qual manifestació Mefistòfeles replica tot rient-se'n: "Den letzten, schlechten, leeren Augenblick, / Der Arme wünscht ihn festzuhalten" ("El moment final, desastrós i buit / el pobre home vol retenir"[10]) (vv. 11589-90).

5. Aquests passatges que narren la fi d'un Faust desesperat davant la mort, ens esclareix quin és el subjecte gramatical del passatge del CEMarag. En realitat, *'Aquell* que a cap moment li digué..." fóra Faust (és a dir, si es vol, Goethe), el qual a cap 'moment' de la seva existènci-

a, a cap instant del seu viure, mai no li va demanar que es parés, excepte a aquell instant o moment que el duia i el menà a la mort. És a dir, el subjecte d'aquella frase maragalliana és Faust, però el complement del verb 'dir' no és altre que 'moment' (el 'Augenblick' del text alemany).[11] Degut a aquesta interpretació, bé es podria sostindre que el CEMarag és una repulsa del *Faust*, la repulsa del 'pobre' Faust (el 'der Arme' del text alemany) per part de l'home mediterrani que sap a tothora gaudir del sol, del mar i de les muntanyes i que no vol "més cel que aquest cel blau." En fi, el "Cant Espiritual" de Maragall, aquell cant estructuralment emparentat al "Cant Espirirual" d'Ausiàs March, adquireix una nova dimensió artística i espiritual en referir-se a un personatge i a una obra de transcendència universal.

Center for Catalan Studies
The Catholic University of America
Washington, DC 20064

NOTES FINALS

[1] Treiem els textes adduïts de J. M. Castellet i J. Molas, *Antologia general de la poesia catalana* (Barcelona: Edicions 62,1979).

[2] Anotem que dos 4-8 es presenten al final de la composició, donant, amb el trencament de la norma predominant, un fort aire dramàtic.

[3] Cal indicar que, a part aquests tres tipus ben diferenciats, hi ha així mateix en el CEMarch un petit número (3,092%) de casos de difícil classificació.

[4] Com a punt de referència podríem assenyalar que en el "Sum Veris" de Verdaguer, les tonalitats -o- i -u- aconsegueixen un 20,168% i un 11,764%, mentre que, dins el timbre general vocàlic, -o- i -u- estan representats per un elevat 22,372% i 11,525% respectivament (16,843% i 7,019% dins el sistema de les cinc composicions que conjuntament analitzem).

[5] Considerem la frase com el contingut entre dues pauses fortes, marcades per un punt (o els seus equivalents, els signes d'admiració i d'interrogació) o un punt i coma.

[6] Utilitzem el programa creat per Louis i Robert Ule, adaptant-lo a les exigències del català.

[7] Deduïm ja els casos de 'ser/ésser' en calitat de localització, que en el CEMarag adquireixen un 0,787%.

[8] Traducció de l'autor.

[9] Idem.

[10] Idem.

[11] Aquesta interpretació pot veure's ja apuntada en l'article de la meva malaurada alumna Maria Guitart i Ribas, la qual honestament me l'atribueix. "Faust and the 'Cant Espiritual'" *Catalan Review* III,ii (July, 1989): 85-97. Ara bé, no sé per quina raó els passatges que addueix no són pas els més escaients.

TWO
CONTEMPORARY
CATALAN POETS
IN TRANSLATION

TWENTY SEVEN POEMS
—OF GOLD, OF SILVER AND OF TIN

(VINT-I-SET POEMES EN TRES TEMPS)[1]

by

Miquel Martí i Pol

Translated by

Elaine Marie Lilly

---

[1] Published in Barcelona by Edicions 62, in 1972.
Miquel Martí i Pol, 1972, sota llicéncia d'Edicions 62, S.A.

Prologue

Time hangs from multiple pins.
The first is of gold;
the second of silver;
the third of tin;
and the others I don't know.
Behind each door
there are people who shake jinglebells
right at the tempting rim
of the words.

Look at me carefully: I am the other.
Lame in both feet,
sullen and solitary.
I've come from nowhere
and I write to survive.
I retrace my steps
because I don't know any shortcuts.
I take up old habits.
If I still could, I'd lie
in the scattered clearings
with dark-skinned girls.

But I've grown up
and someone filled my blood
full of glass.
Look at me carefully: I limp.
I have nothing except
the voice that represents me.
I pour out words
and the words purify me.

I'll emerge from myself the day
that a whirlwind
dries my eyes. This struggle,
with its towering, fiery swords,
upholds me
in the face of fears and dreams.
Look at me carefully;
Look at me carefully: I am the other.

I don't ask for much:
to be able to speak without disguising my voice;
to walk without crutches;
to make love without having to ask permission;
to write on a page without ruled lines.

Or, if that seems too much:
to write without having to disguise my voice;
to walk without ruled lines;
to speak without having to ask permission;
to make love without crutches.

Or, if that seems too much:
to make love without having to disguise my voice;
to write without crutches;
to walk without having to ask permission;
to be able to speak without ruled lines.

Or, if that seems too much...

This comes to us from long ago:
                    [from the great-great-grandfather,
maybe, who cultivated another's fields with primitive tools,
or from the grandmother who worked as a servant girl
and said "m'lady" to her mistress.
I mean this affection freely offered,
this sickly taste of earth on the lips
and the meekness of a frightened dog
deep in the eyes.
This comes to us from long ago;
and the cold in the marrow of the bones,
the glass in the blood and the little mirror
that distorts the image.
They're symbols transmitted through life,
like a sickness,
uprooted only by a downpour
that cleanses the guts.
This comes to us from long ago:
                    [from great-great-grandfather,
maybe, or farther back.

Sometimes,
on a normal afternoon,
tenderness saturates the words
and the softest drizzle
makes flowers explode in the marshes
and grass grow on the hillsides.
Then,
it's easy to tumble
down a slope of
dutifully disinfected words
and find out,
between gulps of coffee,
that in some far-off country
the war still persists
and people die of hunger.
At that point, one exclaims easily:
what sons-of-bitches men are!
Sometimes, I tell you,
the tenderness saturates the words.

Two old men who are climbing the stairs
are saying that winter used to be longer.
Longer than that is your hair, and dense
like the letters of the newspaper
that says the B-52's, yesterday,
established a new record for combat actions in Indo-China,
where the sky is maybe blue
like the ribbon on the gondolier's hat
that I've put away in I don't know which closet,
or like the underwear I can see hanging
on that old balcony right in front of the house,
old like the two men who, now,
are climbing, step by step, the stairs.

Those who every Sunday, seated in automobiles,
go by in a steady stream on the highway,
go from the seacoast to the shade of the woods,
or down the mountain to the sun on the beaches.
They all feel their muscles tightened by the week
of fear and of solitude they've come through
and they scrutinize the horizon, like the people of the great
exoduses, confronting the solitude and the fear that wait for
them. Each automobile is an enclosed box,
an unreal world, a fortress,
and the people that inhabit it are sullen and bitter.
Looking at them from the beautiful midpoint of an immense
afternoon, intoxicating with colors and shapes,
I ask that you take note of their anguish.

This man who sits in front of his house
has accumulated memories the thickness of a coin
and he rots slowly, as if he were a leaf.
For a long time the mastiffs have chased
the girls with firm breasts and tender gazes;
for a long time on the restless hump of the waters,
on the threads of the wind, with papers and proclamations,
everywhere the bosses have sterilized the weak.
This man who sits in front of his house
has bought, on installments, a future made of tinfoil;
he is a castrated stud with his chest full of scabs,
who slouches grotesquely in front of the tender young girls
and washes his feet very little so as not to waste his inheritance.
This man of clay, when the rain erodes him,
will barely have time to take off his shoes
and rough out with his hands a great gesture of surprise.
Tadpoles will grow in the puddle he'll make.

This poem is a
sun of braided straw,
plucked from the bottom of a well
exactly at midafternoon.
The well has long been dry;
the people drink other waters.
From time to time, someone
peeks over the edge and leaves.
At the deepest part of the well
seven spiders make their nests.
They weave, patiently,
suns of braided straw.
If a little wind blows,
the suns raise up in the air.
When they rise out of the well,
the afternoon is much brighter.
This poem is a sun of braided straw.

Hang a sheet on the wall. Move
your hands in front of the lamp,
and the shadow will serve as
a very strange mirror.
If you manage
to read between the signs and symbols,
the new insights will terrify you.

It must have been a clouded May,
with hazy afternoons that wrap
heavily around the muscles;
a milky May, loaded with presentiment.
Ai! if we had known how to read the signals:
the salt, the rocks,
the sand or, maybe, the wind...our knees
would have been shaking!
But life, which detaches itself
and deforms us, strikes with treachery.
Then, the whole bundle of tenderness
nurtures the clumps of algae
that cause idleness,
and subtle alcohols create scales of onyx
in the intestines.
What good does it do to know the weather?
Nothing is left of the years
except a bitter taste that forms a crust
inside the stubborn mouth that chews on
roots, memories, and an occasional blade of green grass.
We have a bland palate and, outside,
it's a milky May, once again.

With the taste of green plums
and soft fuzz on your cheeks...
This is almost how years ago
the same image appeared to you,
maybe because at the time you balanced
in a false equilibrium, on both feet.
Now you know that there is this narrow path
across a spectrum of shapes and colors
that takes you back to a well-known beach.
Well then, as tenderly as you can, place
your foot on each grain of sand.
Captivated like a child
studying the nearest hills, as if they were
horizons of an undiscovered land.
And don't be troubled that the deep thunder of the sea
barely reaches your ears.

Before any plans of roses or of wind.
Even before the currents and the tides,
when my index finger painstakingly traced
the outline of your breasts,
maybe the rain wouldn't have softened
our gums like now.
If we had loved each other with enough fury
—although of course the poor are not permitted such excesses—
maybe now we'd have, all to ourselves,
an island with golden beaches and a gleaming white house.
But our teeth have rotted, bit by bit,
from so much chewing without desire;
and as we (still!) pick off
the wilted gladiola blossoms,
our hands tremble with disgust, tenderness...

This waiting has the force of water,
the expectation of the body tense before love.
Dolphins slip along the skin of memory;
which calms itself and suddenly,

                    [it seems the tides have stopped.
A steep street and the arch of a body that bends
to delicately pull up the root of memory.
This opaqueness doesn't torment you as much,
nor these hands, now nearly translucent
like the pages of a book that has been read many times.
In the summer clouds you'll hang up your eyes
so that the depths of your gaze will be washed
and your eyes will be clear when the sun is high again.

This happened in the fall and the words
revealed nothing.
It had to be a benign afternoon
so that no gesture could be exaggerated or sterile.
You said: that the sun sets slowly
and how the night heals the space between the leaves.
And you were quiet, afterwards.
Savoring the silence is a very
discreet way of loving. The hands
that trace words,
and the sun-filled eyes, and the sighs so near.
Now it won't be necessary, from this moment on,
to look back any further.

It came out of the clouds. Has it been restored to us
by some benevolent little god or, maybe,
the deep, secret sigh of the earth?
Look at the streets, so clean at this hour.
All is well and good, and a dog that passes
has eyes as clear as two drops of water.

Every morning, before you leave your house,
wash your eyes with distilled water
and rub your wrinkles with sandpaper.
Like the fish that stubbornly leaps the river,
throwing himself at it, may the water not stop you;
and learn well the shape of each rock.
Every morning, before you leave your house,
gulp the wind at an open window,
chew roots of bitter herbs,
perfume your armpits with lemon
and scrub your teeth and nails
so that, when the moon changes
—and it will change, my friend, don't doubt that!—
you won't need patches or ointments
to withstand the force of the new tides.

How little resonance life has nowadays,
the flowers made of stone,
the boats off their moorings!
How little resonance, what a slow death!
If it were still the era of roosters on the rooftops
and women in the doorways, we could
try once again to throw open the windows,
to abandon this sinister corridor,
to love each other furiously,
to kill the dragon with the seven heads
and free the princesses.
But we have so pawned our inheritance
that the wind, if it blows, now only catches
the tips of our hair,
and nostalgia has become, in the end,
a useless luxury.
How little resonance life has nowadays!

Of myself I know very little. Maybe
that's why even though I now could
sell this body, for what it's worth,
I cannot slice myself into pieces.

A dog barks outside
and the wind squeezes through the doors.
It will make the reeds whistle,
if that spot near the water is still the same as before.

There is no present:
all paths are memory or inquiry.

The most difficult thing, then, is to survive
with shards of glass in your guts,
with lead instead of blood in your veins.
To survive: tie your shoes,
work, make love, read poems,
watch people get old, sing out loud
with shards of glass in your guts
and lead, instead of blood, in your veins,
without tearing your eyes out, without shattering
the small, subtle mirrors of the dream
and squealing like a pig, from fear or envy.

Maybe we would be less sullen
if we didn't know we were confined inside a
small, windowless room full of dust
and old furniture, with piles of paper;
if each step we take didn't raise echoes
of obscure and sinister presences,
if we could call out without fear or shame.
Maybe we would learn to smile
and we wouldn't damage our nails so much,
clawing at walls, while they. outside,
ring bells, make proclamations,
maintain order, screw us all...

Ai! What a heavy weight I feel in my muscles,
thanks to these people who work only to
secure a solid and stable future
and who age, impatient and resentful,
before the persistent wickedness of mankind.
These talkative and eager people
who, without apparent effort,
separate good from evil
and with a heavy, scolding index finger
deal out punishment and hatred.
These tenacious people, who do business
and defend it arrogantly, and bit by bit
become ugly and oppressive and sad...
Ai! What a heavy weight;
what a bad taste in the mouth!

You remember almost nothing
of the woods, that were so close before;
and, all the same, it forms part of your
personal history.
To forget is also to live.
Now it is time again
to sit on stone benches,
fix your eyes on midafternoon,
wash your hands
in rainwater.
The downpour will come again.
It is the time of tender wheat and of salt.
Turn your face to the wind and, little by little,
you'll feel how your skin unwrinkles.

Ah, how beautiful it would have been to grow up
without this enormous weight on the shoulders,
without this great nuisance inside the mouth,
in a white house, near the sea,
with the windows always open.
How beautiful to have been able to
cultivate the earth, write verses,
meet people, attract girls
with smooth muscles and sharp teeth.
We wouldn't find it
indecent or cowardly now to sit in the clearings
and wait for the flowering of the roses,
and we wouldn't have such red eyes,
nor dry lips, nor this scratchy voice.
Moss wouldn't grow now
in the marrow of our bones,
if we had been able to live without this
great nuisance inside the mouth,
without this enormous weight on the shoulders.

Can one still speak with fire the name of this country
with so many aggressive beasts that never split
their hooves so as not to lose their privileges?
Where is the sea that has no boats?
And why are so many people in the doorways?
No rooster sings out the exact hour,
and the clocks are eyes without pupils.
If I went to the rooftop, would you listen to me?
Now is the hour of lightning, but the rain
must be far away; the waiting tires us.
We can put up awnings beneath the porches
and protect memories from the rain. Hands are moving
like leaves in the woods. Where are the woods?
And, with so much mud, will there be any paths?
Whoever has hope should hang it out
on the balcony over the street. Slow death,
from fear or bad faith, they call life.
To survive we squander our inheritance
and to see things more clearly we lift our eyes
at each streetcorner.

If I were you, I'd try on again
that sweater
with the leather elbow patches
and I'd go back and take the canary
off the window ledge.
One never knows, the winds...
And I've heard it said that words,
if one airs them out,
burst with more force inside the mouth.
I'd open the door to the street
and maybe I'd even go for a walk
up and down the sidewalk,
with that wry, challenging air
you had when you looked in the mirror with pride
at your well-behaved body.
If you look carefully you'll notice that cloudbursts
only carry away with them superfluous soil.

You can turn the calendar backwards:
every number, a secret.
You can, with effort, walk backwards,
wear dark glasses all day long,
read from right to left.
Apparently unrooted,
you'll become a surreal copy
of your real self;
a false reproduction.
And after all, relentless death
will harvest your memories,
which you call future.
Where can you go, ox, where you won't have to plow?

This rumble that you hear is not the rain.
It's been a long time since it rained.
The springs have gone dry and the dust is getting thick
in the streets and the houses.

This rumble that you hear is not the wind.
They've outlawed the wind so that it won't raise
the dust that is everywhere
and make the air—they say—unbreathable.

This rumble that you hear is not words.
They've prohibited words
so they don't endanger
the fragile immobility of the air.

This rumble that you hear is not thoughts.
They've been prohibited so that they don't create
a necessity to speak
causing, inevitably, the catastrophe.

And, nonetheless, the rumble still persists.

LIPS THAT DANCE

(LLAVIS QUE DANSEN)[1]

by

Olga Xirinacs

Translated by

Hillary J. Gardner

[1] Published in Barcelona by Edicions Proa, in 1987
Olga Xirinacs, 1987, sota llicéncia d'Enciclopèdia Catalana, S.A.

Foreword

"I've been on the look out for the horizon to the end of the seas, as if from there came certainty."

This is a fragment from the first poem in this book and a very habitual gesture of mine that I often note down in my afternoon diary. Magnificently privileged, I always have the sea within eyes' reach. For me, it is the beginning and end of adventure, the start of a voyage and the return; in between there lies the immense solitude of the spirit subjected to time's routine passing. It is because of this that I am now pleased to share to the reader some of what I found and expressed in poems during the course of the years.

"...as if from there came certainty." Certainty of what? Only of the passing of time. From here the references to some of the months of the year that, despite of the existential anguish and human tragedies generated by our limitations, always carry the unifying elements that help us get over and minimize these limits: roses, tulips, chrysanthemums and coffee tables in the city; heather, gulls, the port and seaweed on the coast; the satiated womb of the earth and the ripening berries in the fields and woods; and the beautiful September clouds, the most loved month of all for the spirit it returns to nature.

In regards to skin: this "warm geography of the body," object of love and contemplation from life's beginning, is admired here with the deep feeling born from recognizing it as fragile and fleeting, and with the due surprise of one who finds it hard to watch its decay and would halt its passing with a poem.

Bare skin may be caressed by lips and hands and also a light breath with which perfumers, in a remote invention, have wanted to seduce and condition the sense of smell. The suggestive names of perfumes can, and do, adapt to the skin of a poem and clothe it.

In Virgil we find the rural element as a pretext for introducing the spiritual richness of the author and his poet friends in a glowing Arcady. The happy parenthesis of nature's song opens, as an escape, in an epoch of crises and wars. The Eclogues sing of love and enmity, playing with the gods and inviting one to taste life's joy, that which should be as common as blood and water, within us and everlasting.

For, certain as twilight, at the end of the day and time there is one who speaks of shipwrecks. And if we have not attained a joy in living—subtle, glorious and wild—then for certain, by contrast, we will not be spared such a wreck.

I would like to be able to communicate this vital pleasure and to construct, as a way of holding onto it, a sumptuous home. At times our palaces are made only of words, we wish they were beautiful, we poets have nothing else. Perhaps, through poems, someone else will realize joy exists and is certain. I have found this certainty in looking at the sea and in starting my voyage.

The Satiated Land

—By way of introduction

I had to wait. To see the yucca bloom,
right at the end of summer, a risen torch, white;
may the birds quiet down in the trees
and the sun set over a godless sea.

I had to wait. And once gone
the arid summer days,
to return to the word like to an old flame
or to a privilege long wished for.
I've been on the look out for the horizon to the end of the
[seas,
as if from there came certainty.
I've found the reason for the silence on hand,
the time of being aged gets near,
when the lover's passing through mild mists
crosses this September and accompanies me.
Plenitude of berries, of silk dresses,
of metal fires and of trapped blood
that has forgotten pain.
The land, satiated, shows off a body entirely bare.

I will prepare for autumn's entrance
so that winter's days, here in the city,
are pleasant for me. I will count the pauses
of nameless books; I will look at myself in the mirror
and recognize you, word-image
gone over with my lips, desired,
forgotten moon in the gods' universe.

From the Sea You Will Rise like the Mist

"...a god has given me this ease..."
—**Virgil,** Eclogue 1

September advances with you, in love with mist,
announcing itself with a melancholic touch,
making the first smile over the fields
like one surveying a house, closed up,
where, at summer's arrival, he was happy.
Poet in love with forgotten images
will tell you it is beautiful—September,
crowned with strawberry trees,
like a lover impatient for you.
Bee-eaters sing and the air is sweet
when the berries ripen,
and the moss prepares
the nocturnal visitors' stay.
Still, the afternoon inflames my desire
for the love that nears:
from the sea you will rise like the mist
to fall asleep with me.
September, the one of returns
to old and new dwellings,
where my eyes' path over books
and the conversation between your lips
stops for a moment in the flames
and revives the colors of disquiet.

Not time, but rest, I would
like to make us eternal.

Meditation for the Passing of May into June

> *"Oh, many times, oh charming words*
> *she's spoke to me, my Galatea!*
> *Whisper a few, a few of them,*
> *you breezes, into heaven's ear!"*
> —**Virgil,** Eclogue 3

We are entering June, you tell me, and I don't listen
because with my hands, afflicted, on the paper
I am thinking of those adolescent summers
and of this June that soon will separate me
from the wheat fields that were sown forever
—from the old paths among the vines,
from the evening silence in the hills,
when the sky and land were one.

There are no benevolent archangels; images
flee a distant sky
and now my land is already another.
If I look at you, this silence of your eyes
brings back to me the weeping acacia,
the water of a storm and silk pillows,
the hoisted lamp, the nocturnal music,
the hidden notebooks and the elegy
to our brief bodies, abandoned
in any incandescent landscape.

June is arriving and we'll find it beautiful
because you are my land and my wheat

and my nightly disquiet and my wine and honey.
There is, in the background of the picture, the perspective
of another June overhead, without weight,
shadow of an evanescent paradise.

Meditation for a June Night

> *"Yet surely you could rest with me tonight and sleep*
> *On a bed of green leaves here? You're welcome to taste my mellow*
> *Apples, my floury chestnuts, my ample stock of cheese. "*
> —**Virgil**, Eclogue 1

The day bent to contemplate
your body between the roses in a light that wept,
velvet on velvet, the pleasure
of that unshed blood grew.
The air steadied itself on the silence
steered by desire coming into port.
The flowers picked in the morning lowered
their proud plant spears, watching over
magic fires in the solitude
of the room's white walls.

I write words I don't want to die,
born from an earth without a name.
I say them one by one, whispering,
in the repose of time conquering us.
On the fiery lips of June there is
a poem kissing you slowly.

One June Day

> *"Look at how the round and ponderous globe bows to salute you,*
> *The lands, the stretching leagues of sea, the unplumbed sky!*
> *Look how the whole creation exults in the age to come!*
> *If but the closing days of a long life were prolonged*
> *For me, and I with breath enough to tell your story..."*
> —**Virgil**, Eclogue 4

"Time passes, lady, time passes..."
Where is the boat we hoped for one afternoon?
Who knows the waters it has plowed, or the exotic ports.
The stars have seen it at night as it went by
and mistook it for a fallen dream.
Let's leave behind all this light, all these dreams,
that the sea, on moonlit nights, explains,
like one showing off a case of diamonds,
crowns, slippers, bridal necklaces,
and words spoken and unspoken also,
and flowers and hands that opened and closed.
Love that didn't come, love that left
and small afternoon paradises
that are then aren't, that float, iridescent, as fragile
as the air that makes them fall to the sea, hurrying,
because the boat is passing—the ship that one day
we saw coming in from afar. That arrived. That is leaving us.

Meditation for the Middle of June

> *"What, oh what can I do to reward you for such singing?*
> *Sweeter it was to me than a south wind's rising murmur*
> *Or the rhythmic drumming of waves on a beach..."*
> —**Virgil,** Eclogue 5

June love begins with the desire
of a sea of adventure, not so far away
that we forget the city, glass urn,
sepulcher of gods and infants
that we were for a time. June love
is a love that arrives like waves,
like squadrons of gulls each evening:
having already mastered the sea heights,
they return to the hideout to dream
of coves, rocks and moons, the barking
of dogs on the beach and the beat
of the lovers' sex between the dunes.

Water Is Near

"Let the wild waves pound the shore, and come to me..."
—**Virgil,** Eclogue 9

Water is near, now the sea is waking,
immense surface, long skin
where caprice marks new routes
so that you may navigate them.

You open your hands, the sun is all here,
September sun with the taste of pale clouds,
skin of a summer that flees without recall
of so many days with you.

The wind makes the curtains move still
softly, the trees and the birds;
salt enters until it touches lips
so that you may taste.

Transparent hours, forgotten words,
return to land from the sea. A beautiful journey
has brought them here from a country
we waited for in dreams.

Hands on Wood

> *"Ash queens in woods, and stone-pine in gardens,*
> *by streams the poplar, on heights the fir-tree:*
> *If Lycidas only were with me more often,*
> *ash-tree and pine would be nothing to me. "*
> —**Virgil,** Eclogue 7

It is the hour of hands on wood
—bodies dead and alive rest there—
we count the grains, go over the knots,
fir, willow, cherry,
walnut, olive, oak, pine and mahogany,
pungent wood, warm, worked
by hands that will not know us.

In the window you have basil,
on the bed a bouquet of dried flowers,
and broom on the glass table.
The china reflects your eyes,
I see there pollen of mallow
and the flight of bees.
When our bare feet make the wood creak,
no one will take from us the sky we have
tied to the headboard.

Meditation for When Summer Begins

> *"What an inspired poet you are! To me, your singing*
> *Is good as a sleep on the grass to a tired man..."*
> —**Virgil,** Eclogue 5

Cherry season is not yet over,
nor the one of ladies with roses on their breasts;
the flock of crows crosses the border
and they a splendid light has dressed.

The roses will languish on street corners,
without cries the fruit will start its descent,
words on my fingers will founder,
and the flight of birds through fires be spent.

"More Fair Than Pale Ivy..."

> *"More sweet than thyme, more fair than pale ivy,*
> *more white than swans you are to me..."*
> —**Virgil,** Eclogue 7

I describe again for you the wild rose
and the light of a morning in half fog
—so many years growing, dying, yet always new.
But I cannot describe for you the path
of hands over the dream,
because the dream is the body and the hand
and the word that makes them live.
Beauty by day or by night, what of it,
if thought, like air, moves its hands
in secret dwellings without names?
I do not dare write of shades of light
or of the kiss that makes its way,
for letters make limits
and words, walls.
On your world the dream is always new
as are your eyes on me.

Meditation Right in the Middle of Summer

> *...we shall reach town, don't worry;*
> *Or if there's a fear the night may turn rainy,*
> *we can press on,*
> *Singing as we go, a song lightens a long road.* "
> **-Virgil**, Eclogue 9

It is not death that comes to receive us;
today we slowly descend the staircase
of a midday asleep in amphoras.
Life vainly leads us
to agonize in forgotten rooms.
Nor is it spirit that shows us the tomb,
but eyes that, fearfully, rejected shadows.
We have salt on our lips
and on our hands rust from antique keys,
custody of forgotten loves.
Time lived with you is not a space
made from empty sepulchers.
Sunlight on your hair vanishes like a kiss
on a beloved body
and so will meaning and essence
when we climb the city streets.
There is a flight of torturous twins
and a clear light sleeping in the pines;
time past that falls like rain
that does not forget land,
like your eyes weeping in the afternoon,
transparent resin,
density that flows in a body that is bare.

October Walk

"...How tranquil my bones would rest,
If over them your reed-pipes were making my love
immortal!"
—**Virgil**, Eclogue 10

Distinct smell of the elevated land,
when an acacia shudders with you
because the October air awaited you.
The beach, backing off, feels the waves
as they cover it, threatening and evasive;
how, from afar, it brings the broken voice
of dead fish and the torn clothing
of an unknown drowned man.
The rainwater seeks its paths,
October paths, open, forgotten stone
of a lost land, dragged
between dead hazelnuts and bare trees.

I feel your skin and the first fire
accompanies afternoons at home.
There are clouds aloft, thin lips
in love and numb, drinking up silences
of beautiful solitude, frozen,
that the fervor of kisses does not reach,
nor the smell of new smoke, nor the old flavor
of wine that one sips slowly, nor the pleasure
of the fleeing light, so brief, so far away.

Collapse on the Grass

> *"All nature smiles, but it handsome Alexis*
> *goes from these hills, even the streams may run dry."*
> —**Virgil**, Eclogue 7

One day we collapsed on the grass:
it was the first day, everything still unnamed,
not even death existed.
From lost heights I descended to valleys,
the mist lifted, like sleep
from shut eyelids.
Cabins, smoke, the stone path,
the cherry blossom, the flock of sheep, the magpies
—all came out of the shadows and the forgotten
like bare touch growing on the day's skin.
The first dreams came true
and disappeared like water from leaves
under the midday sun, with the light breezes.
It was the time of collapse on the grass,
the exact hour when lips forgot
the poems they had half begun.
Colors conquered shadows
—lively flames against the cold of the north
and voice against the walls of silence.

Imitation of Night

> *"Love conquers all. We also give ourselves up to Love!"*
> —**Virgil**, Eclogue 10

Only the light in your eyes and the shadows on our bodies.
The baked earth has taken on its color,
devoured by late evening fires.
Now it is night, although shadows
let pass, like a glance,
an uncertain brightness, shaky fingers
of a hand that celebrates in silence
the initiation of night.

After the fire, hands are mist,
born near water among the bracken
and the feline steps of genets;
they are silk veils, they slip and please,
conjurers of night, they hide,
they disappear, vanished in the intent
of assaying the last game, capturing prey,
drinking their fill one more time until the light,
hard and jealous, scatters mirages.

> *"Cruel Alexis, can my sad airs mean nothing to you?*
> *No pity for me? One day you'll drive me to my death."*
> -**Virgil**, Éclogue 2

The rain falls hard
on the dry palms.
Waves bring back bitter water to me.
I feel the hurt of you
on my deserted skin.
I look for words I haven't said,
they are at the bottom of desire,
their roots lost.
Blood and ice hide the roads,
handfuls of warm feathers huddle
in the forks of trees,
soft, beating.
Someone is rebelling
with the last cry of an anguishing day.
Do you know how the hurt grows
from time without you?

"Rive Gauche"

Time pauses within the room
over the precise volumes of your body
as I forget the streets of mid-afternoon.
Thick, white magnolia leaves
are flowered silk in the repose
of your eyes long yearned for.
Every window changes color
when the hours, gently, fall;
everything dies from within, at each turn
images are hidden, hold
the intensity of change on lovers.
There are pauses in the stone and wood,
the repose of an inner architecture.
It is not the pause of bodies or of air.
When desire makes its way again,
the city takes on colors of green glass,
once again a fleeting light grows,
pleasure tightens on the skin, and is lost.

"Lumière"

Poem dancing to a waltz by Erik Satie

Who proposed a dance this afternoon?
In the afternoon there's music hung
beneath the air of a kiss, on the skin,
kisses that come and go, and the charm
of the notes of glass.
The sun dances in the drinks,
hands and lips dance,
and Erik Satie smiles from a piano
that is strolling through the clouds.
New music, where lovers, defeated,
smile at Satie, who waltzes in a sky
of immortal clarity.
The sun wounds the eyes and is like a cry
that goes through crystal and is lost at the bottom
of the body's shadows.
Later, Satie, longing will come. Later.
And, from a sad piano, you tell us about it.

"Arpège"

The golden skin stretches north and south,
warm geography of the body.
The sun has come through it in auriferous shades,
it is the skin that beats in silence; when I listen to it
I appreciate subtle variations
born deep in one's interior.
Its aura is vast, concentrated,
the entire universe throbs inside
and irradiates to infinite distances:
the falling star takes with it, in a brief flight,
its splendid color to its death.
The skin comes from a primal world
that one day, by chance,
someone discovered but did not name.

"L'heure bleue"

October love, pale,
yours is a naked adolescent,
sincere, new, compressed.
You have a world of glass spells
behind your eyes.
Water, pollen, the blond bees' flight,
shadow your skin,
you are grazing land for lips and hands,
desire for a long silence you ignored.
Love is yours, all yours,
impatience belongs to you
and the feverish kiss that will open your teeth,
delta of hidden waters.
If life sets upon you,
howling, bitten, such a white love:
you will be broken by burning cracks,
gaping china,
crevice without blood,
October love, unfrozen, open.

"Clandestine"

The wind was dying on the windows,
and the room was bare.
We had no roofs nor doors,
but you didn't get wet in the rain.
Nor silk bedspreads, nor curtains,
but you were never cold.
You, like ivory, were so beautiful
that no shadow,
swan feather, mimosa flower,
not even a single verse or word
was to touch you. On you,
only the poet's stare.

"Eau folle" (1)

Masks in the port

Carnival afternoon. When it gets dark
the white-robed angel
lights colored sparks,
and gray-glass eyes reflect
lively sparkler stars.
Sailors' voices climbing
the city streets come closer.
Somebody blue-eyed
watches how the floats pass;
the silk dragging like fog
folded over the horizon, red and blue,
yellow and pink, no wind.
The route is the street, and the port, the night.
Later everything is undone, the air takes
away the streamers and voices. The sailors
have drunk to the memory of a room
with windows lost to the north.

"Eau folle" (2)

Masks in the port

Love hides in the mist,
under the waters, by the side of a boat;
a piece of silk hides it, a bundle of feathers,
a net with scales
or a black mask.
A sparkler sheds light on it,
a street breaks it up, a window,
a crane, the docks, a wall,
the very air that passes through
the wings of doves,
that kisses his hair, that takes away his body,
that looks, listens, stays quiet,
that sails and is lost.

"L'air du temps"

It was very early in the morning. I could hear the water
on the little lake. I could sense the solitude
gilded by my eyes' fog,
still sleepy, like the horizon and the sea.
My dreams had left you
gradually, the way a slow ship
leaves port.
I don't want anything else. It is all held up here,
this bare silence prepares the day.
The absence of your body is a pause
that falls in the sweet quiet
of knowing and feeling. And I listen to the water
thresh the morning.

"Quelques fleurs"

They were picked one sharp and white
morning in May. They were white too
and made green shadows, transparent
like water on a satiated lawn.
One by one they were chosen
to hold your body in the silence,
blossoming hands in slow descent.
One by one they drew near, tenderly,
to fall on you like a rain a sunny sky
did not predict. Flowers in your hands
and on your breast, kissing your skin,
shivered with you, covered you, clearly,
to delight in the life you gave to them.

"Magie Noire"

Nocturnal island

Between my hands grows a black island,
nocturnal island that begins to live
when evening unfolds.
At the tips of my fingers are jungle spaces,
pulps with a pleasant feel, fruitful,
that the day's pause has ripened.
At night, the black island begins
imprecise plant-like motions.
Its silence vibrates under the water
of secret currents.
Narcissi flower in the eye of narcissi
and the black island trembles when
anyone, among the shadows, ventures there.

"Crêpe de Chine"

Hands on paper

I took up a blank sheet of paper to draw some hands.
I had thought of them that evening
when the glass doors opened and all dreams
dressed in blue between conversations.
They were winter days and the paper demanded hands from me,
but the inclement cold delayed the light.
Spring came with the melting of peaks
over the high valleys. The snow was shaken on the
                              [mountains.
A dead river reached to where we were
thirsty from rain. The grass grew bitter and without seed.
But there were books in the study and a clearer light
and coffee steamed on the tables in bars.
Days ripened and a denser color
lit the skin under the sun, the sky burned
and the nights emptied into the sea
drowning desire in silence.
Still the sheet, all white, demanded of me
hands on paper.
The stillness of the afternoon grew,
time adapted to the world like silk to skin,
it was September and shadows were arriving, lamp shades,
                              [topaz,
a long rush of joy was fastened with silver pins.
On the paper were born two hands
the color of the afternoon.

"And of a sudden the journey
resumes
like after a shipwreck
a surviving
sea wolf"
-G. Ungaretti, Shipwrecks

I run my hand over a poem by Ungaretti
not to turn the page, not yet.
But because it is necessary to live the new
meaning in the old words, to accept
the shipwrecks of every day.
And I see the hand that traces a lost course
where afternoon shadows gather,
where the road back is erased,
that has given up to the wind like a ship off course.
I am the sea and the salt from my crying.

The Last Afternoon Sun

*"I find myself
abandoned in infinity"*
—G. Ungaretti, Shipwrecks

Dunes and quiet water, desolate.
Water dies between clots of captured blood.
Over the decomposed, uninhabited land,
neither gulls nor algae. The last sun
unfolds its shroud from the north
over a sea of agony. All shadows
lay their funeral tapestry on the sky:
a landscape unknown to me.
As the sun that takes my life is unknown to me,
as is this terrible battle that separates me
from the time I have already lost. I didn't know
that the water was so dark. I'm wounded
by a death that chases me down, vengeful.

The Red Tulips' Glory

> *"We'll see our love lie back*
> *like the evening"*
> **-G. Ungaretti**, Shipwrecks

They opened like the day, the sea watched them.
The moment of their blooming was so beautiful,
like iridescent light on pupils. It was twelve o'clock
sharp, hour of gods, when I discovered a poet;
and we weren't gods, though well we wanted to be.
Because if this tall bouquet of flowers
has seen glory, has dressed in light,
little by little time has snuffed them
and slowly bent the stems
to spread their fires on the land
from which they had been born but did not know.
Now that a dream of descent guides them,
I close my eyes with them and we forget
the fire of midday on the winter sky.

> *"But my cries*
> *wound*
> *like lightning bolts*
> *the faint bell*
> *of the sky.*
> *They come crashing down*
> *terrified"*
> **-G. Ungaretti,** Shipwrecks

There's something to the afternoon
that makes it return always
as if someone expected it or wanted it.
There's something to the afternoon:
more than a flight of gulls,
or the branch of a tree or the weeping
of the sea mists.
There's the sky over the afternoon,
which has brought it, nothing stops it—
imposing itself like an inopportune host,
changing the color of my hours,
taking the light from my eyes. When
the afternoon brings you near and sends you away,
blurred flight I've soon lost track of,
I find the immense solitude
of night and of emptiness, like a dead star
wandering imprecise routes.
I fear the afternoon that's taken you, that takes me
towards an oblivion with no return, no dawn.

*"In the dark
with frozen
hands
I perceive
my face"*
-G. Ungaretti, Shipwrecks

I have my hands on my lap.
Now I take a piece of paper and hold a pencil.
I don't have anything but a blank page.
Words pass by me like the wind,
words come to me like errant gulls,
the northwesterly takes them away, the westerly
brings them closer,
now they are and they aren't.
The page is still blank,
and this pencil moving between my fingers
is as light as a feather.
If you flourish it, he said, *you'll see a ship come
so that you may board.* It was a fairy tale.
I'll write my poems on the sea,
I thought when I believed in it.
*Nobody writes poems on the sea;
on the sea one walks,*
an old fisherman told me, and he knew.
*Barefoot I walked on water,
and all my mates got scared except one
who tried it and drowned.*

I have a page, still totally blank,
and a fear of shipwreck.

"On the moving
edges of
the shadows
you'll be pruned"
-G. Ungaretti, Shipwrecks

The rain comes intermittently in the wood,
the trees are temperamental
and the afternoon roads frosted;
the coming dark has tortured the branches,
and words die like foam
from the sea over rocks.
There is an inventing of skulls
that decompose, getting soft among the algae.
I'm in the wood, the heather has grown pale,
and on my skin I feel lichen from the north.
I'm losing those visions I long for,
and the body, slowly, gives up space
to the furtive moss that advances
in lowly and partial conquests.
I would like to fall asleep on the sand
like a boat, defeated,
forgotten by its sailors.

"On an ocean
of jingling
unexpectedly
another morning floats"
-G. Ungaretti, Shipwrecks

I set free my long desiring of you
and throw an imaginary net into the sea—
threads that shimmer in the air
with the easterly or northwesterly.
Often they arrive soaked with rain,
with messages from stray shipwrecks
or with dreamy songs of happy sailors.
Some sign they will bring me, I hope,
and I listen to the sea that comes in and back
from a long journey without you.

Catalan Studies
Translations and Criticism

The primary goal of this series of translations and scholarly books will be to disseminate Catalan culture more widely in English-speaking academic circles. Although preference will be given to translations and literary criticism, the series will also publish studies addressing other aspects of Catalan culture and civilization. Manuscripts written in English are preferred, but those written in Catalan or Spanish will also be accepted. Two institutions co-sponsor this series: the Center for Catalan Studies at The Catholic University of America and the Pauli Bellet Foundation, both in Washington, D.C.

Authors are requested to submit a letter of inquiry and a one-page abstract, which should give the title and length of the proposed manuscript to:

Dr. Josep M. Solà-Solé, General Editor
Center for Catalan Studies
Department of Modern Languages
The Catholic University of America
Washington, D.C. 20064